CU00793478

SAHB STORY

SAHB STORY

THE TALE OF

MARTIN KIELTY
AUTHORISED BY
ZAL CLEMINSON   CHRIS GLEN
TED McKENNA   HUGH McKENNA

NEIL WILSON PUBLISHING
WWW.NWP.CO.UK

WWW.SAHBSTORY.COM

Neil Wilson Publishing Ltd
303 The Pentagon Centre
36 Washington Street
GLASGOW
G3 8AZ

Tel: 0141-221-1117
Fax: 0141-221-5363
E-mail: info@nwp.co.uk
http://www.nwp.co.uk

© Martin Kielty, 2004

The author has asserted his moral right under the
Design, Patents and Copyright Act, 1988, to be identified
as the Author of this Work.

A catalogue record for this book is available from the British Library.

ISBN 1-903238-77-3 (trade paperback edition)
ISBN 1-903238-88-9 (casebound limited edition)

Typeset in 10 on 13pt Georgia and Helvetica

Designed by Noisewave Media Control
www.noisewave.com

Printed in Poland

CONTENTS

ACKNOWLEDGEMENTS

SAHB Story contains material which appears in Zal's novel, **Hail Vibrania**, published chapter by chapter on the band's website www.sahb.co.uk .

The portrait of Alex on page 163 was painted by **Catherine Heffernan** (hef@almightygrin.com), who explains the work by saying: 'What do you get if you cross a misspent youth with a seven-foot canvas?'

Photography: **Ronnie Anderson**, **Ian Dickson** (ian@late20thcenturyboy.com), **Peter Ball** (sahb@email.com), **Daily Record**, **Ray Conn**, **Martin Kielty** (martin@sahb.co.uk), **Lee Hagan**, **Mike Drew**, **Mandy Hathway**, **Stefan Pawlata**, **Barry McCulloch**. Where uncredited, pictures come from the band's collection. Every effort has been made to establish and respect copyright. Cover photo: Daily Record

Daily Record: Thanks to the editorial and library staff of the Daily Record and Sunday Mail, particularly **Murray** and **Ronnie**, who helped with research. Your input is always appreciated, guys.

Thanks: Firstly, of course, to **Ted**, **Zal**, **Chris**, **Hugh**, **Billy**, **Dave**, and **Eddie** — I hope you enjoyed it as much as I did. Well, more, actually, because you only had to talk while I had to listen... Then the fan club guys, who I rely on for feedback, opinions and input: I'd love to namecheck you all but I'll only miss someone and get into trouble. Still — hi to Lori, Wade, Jeff, Ash, Lindsey, Mandy, Jack and Gerry. Allan Jones and Charles Shaar Murray for covering and caring. Jon Dore and Barry Brightmore for swelling the archives. John Neil Munro and Joe Black for just doing their jobs, but still managing to show how much they mean it. Barry and Keith for helping me deal with Billy and helping him drink. Tom and Miffy at rockingscots.co.uk. All the contributors for volunteering information and content. Frank Morgan for proof reading, and Joe Owens and David Coyle for helping. (What exactly do you mean, pedantic?) The crew at the Solid Rock, the Copy Cat and Fix for keeping the beer flowing. My own dear crew (dear because I'm always buying), Martin Jarvis and Ali Bear. Alec for kickstarting proceedings.

Special thanks to Nick Low for giving me access to his private archive. Anyone who finds themselves quoted here, but doesn't remember talking to me, actually spoke to Nick; which was lucky for you.

Regards to Trudy, Alex and Tyro.

Double-special thanks to Gibby for actually shutting up while I was whining about this project. And to Damien Kielty, Tim Collins, Steve Banaghan and Brian Mackenna, because I said I would.

All the above people helped make this book worth reading. In a departure from the norm, I'd like to make sure they get the blame for any errors or innaccuracies too.

Dedicated to Claire, and many anniversaries to come.

INTRODUCTION

It was a dreich afternoon in Edinburgh when I met John Neil Munro to interview him about his Alex biography. We sat in an old-fashioned wee pub and talked our talk, and as people nearby became aware of our subject matter, John Neil's standing in the pub rose and rose. He ended up with an impressive amount of respect (and drinks) from perfect strangers. I wanted to be like that.

Well, no I didn't, actually, and still don't. You couldn't describe me as an Alex fan. I didn't meet him, and I'm not convinced I would have liked him. Being magnetically attracted to someone isn't the same as loving them, and so I can't promise to have loved Mr Harvey.

I am, however, a SAHB fan. And I'd like to stress the massive difference. There was a magical period of five years, 1972 until 77, when the best frontman in the world performed with the best band in the world. That they – and significantly, he – could not achieve the same successes alone serves to underline how magical those five years were.

Those five years started the day I was born, 29 June 1972. For another coincidence, it's taken just about five years for this here book to make it into the world. The tale has grown in the telling, and it"s not the only thing around here.

My respect and understanding for the utterly singular thing that is SAHB has grown. Time and tide just do not get in the way of how these four guys communicate, even if they haven't seen each other for years. Their bond, and their bond with Alex, is the one and only instance in which the word "awesome" is not hyperbole.

The position of Alex and SAHB in cultural history has grown - there's been something of a rennaisance. Some of that was me, of course (heh) but the re-release of almost everything the guys ever did has been a major event in everyone's lives this side of the word processor. Pity about Fourplay, but we live in hope.

The list of major acts they influence; the people willing to talk about the band and its music; the number of younger folk, hearing their dads' CD remasters, who've become fans; all these statistics are on the up too.

So, to repeat what I've constantly been saying over the years on the website, this book's not about Alex. It's about SAHB, and there's maybe more of a distinction than a lot of people understand. I hope they'll find some of what they're looking for here; but I reckon some people's Alex isn't to be found outside their own hearts.

Meanwhile, as a record of what happens when you offer five Glesga boys unlimited power, and they trade it in to be rock'n'roll stars, I've tried to make sure it's a bit more fun than some of the band biogs you get.

Vambo, as I have observed for some time now, still rool.

Martin Kielty, July 2004

PART ONE

IN THE
BEGINNING

Those relentless
soulful days,
followed by the
grim iron-fisted
riffs...

Zal with Tear Gas
in Nairn, 1969

1 SCOTLAND'S TOMMY STEELE

IT'S 1956 and every teenager in Scotland is looking for a fight. Or at least, that's what the powers-that-be seem to think. Young post-war post-ration Scotland is bored, frustrated and pissed off, and it's venting itself through a satanic new music movement.

That year the newspapers were mad about it. The Daily Record invented a correspondent called 'Pat Roller', who superhumanly patrolled every town and city every weekend, finding horror stories of barnies, slashings, murders and fearsome loud music.

True, there was a lot of bad stuff happening. Some areas of Scotland – notably Glasgow – have only recently shed the dirty desolate image they earned back then. And much of Glasgow was dirty and desolate, like the infamous slums of the Gorbals, on the south bank of the River Clyde: row upon row of decrepit tenements with outside toilets, playing home to far too many impoverished families. A breeding ground for violence and depression – but also for sparks of magic and unbelievable human warmth. There may have been the odd running battle from time to time, but no one ever had to lock their doors.

The kids were bored, and therefore trouble, and now they were paying that there noisy music a lot more attention than their elders would have liked. No one knew what to do about it, because they saw the music as part of the problem – not part of the solution. Perhaps they could have looked at it this way: put a wayward kid in a band and he's still a wayward kid; but he starts to learn about teamwork, because all the instruments have to play together. He learns about management, because the band has to gig, has to rehearse, and has to find transport for the gear. He learns about responsibility, because if he fucks off with the money at the end of the night his mates will kill him.

But if it all goes well, if the band can string a few chords together, tell a story as if they mean it and persuade the audience to believe it too, then imagination kicks in. The kid starts thinking: this is something I can do. If I'm good enough I can get paid for it as well – get paid for doing something I enjoy. Suddenly there's ambition in his life – a goal and a reason – and he doesn't have to build ships to get it. Naturally the powers-that-were couldn't see it that way.

It was a novelty as much for the parents as the children. Both sides of the divide thought the new movement was scary – they only disagreed on how to respond. Hug it or hurt it? When Bill Haley and the Comets arrived in the UK to rock around the country, it was big but it wasn't accepted. The papers told terrible tales of crowd crushes, panics, fights and deaths. But when Haley returned a few months later, no one cared any more. Someone somewhere had been thinking and realised that getting kids into rehearsal rooms and night clubs was better than having them on the streets – there was more money in it for a start – and, hey, this beat thing isn't too bad, you know? You can

Daily Record

Living in socialist poverty in Glasgow during the 1950s

tap your feet to it... 'Pat Roller' faded away and died (although he was recently dug up again), and entertainment correspondent David Gibson stopped writing exclusively about the ballroom scene in the Daily Record and Sunday Mail, and started courting the newfangled racket. The rock'n'roll years had begun.

It must have been a difficult time for the newspapermen, trying to get a handle on the 'latest craze' – cats, combos, zing girls, top, rocking and sorted... as the weekends passed the papers dared more and more slang words, and once or twice even experimented with dropping the 'g' off 'happening', and started to use the stylism 'rock'n'roll' without quotemarks. (Even in the mid-70s some papers hadn't got used to using the abbreviation 'Alex' without a full-stop.)

But the question was, how do we really get cool? How do we stop following the trends and start setting them? The answer appears to have wafted into old minds after two big events. The first took place towards the end of '56 when a David Gibson feature called out for rock'n'roll singers – Glasgow impresario legend Harry Margolis was looking for a 'hip cat' to liven up his ballroom act, and Gibson used his column to appeal for potential stars. By the following week Margolis had to ask people to stop dialling his three-digit phone number, such was the excitement generated.

The second event was in early '57, when a Sunday Mail feature slammed new 'pop star' Tommy Steele, and their letters page exploded with fury. They ran the headline 'In Defence of Tommy Steele', and carefully admitted (without actually admitting) that they'd probably had more letters on this topic than anything else in years. And the great reactionaries reacted: 'Are you Scotland's Tommy Steele?'

The contest ran over a month in Glasgow, Edinburgh, Ayr, Dundee, Kirkcaldy, Aberdeen, Inverness and Dumfries. Over 600 young men (and, we assume, no young women) made it past the auditions to appear in the heats. Singing, dancing, twanging six-strings, they all played to impress a group of people who, on and off, were still claiming the rock'n'roll trend was dying on its feet.

It was April 1957. Dance halls were beginning to hire 'bouncers'. There was outrage over the Scottish Football Association's plans to spend an extra £400 on the World Cup trip, while Scotland lost 2-1 to England at Wembley, and Falkirk won the Cup. Nearly two million shipbuilders and engineers called off a three-week strike after rejecting a paltry ten percent pay rise. The TV and radio licence went up from £1 to £4, but the minimum bus fare was frozen at 2d. A deluxe scooter cost £167, or £177 with an electric starter. Martial law was declared in Jordan. Billy Butlin promised campers their best year ever, while Terry-Thomas bemoaned the loss of his trademark £100 cigarette holder. Lonnie Donegan was at the top of the charts with Cumberland Gap. And Alex Harvey was Scotland's Tommy Steele.

David Gibson proudly introduced the winner: straight off the back streets, a 22-year-old Glasgow boy who'd rebuilt a £3 guitar and used it to beat off opposition from other young Scots with £100 guitars. The Mail was not only delighted to have set an unknown on his path to success; it was pleased that the prize had gone to someone who was obviously 'just an ordinary Glasgow lad.'

Gibson wrote: 'When he was 21 he married his girlfriend, a cinema usherette. The only house they could get was a single-end in Crown Street, a cramped little apartment with walls which showed signs of dampness.'

It was Alex's energy in his rendition of Hound Dog which had attracted the judges. It was Alex's energy which was always going to attract everyone. His belief in the power of storytelling – the ability to generate stunning images without complex stage effects – hailed back to his own early experiences.

Page 10 SUNDAY MAIL, April 28, 1957.

HE IS SCOTLAND'S TOMMY STEELE!

Back streets kid wins stardom chance

Alex Harvey in action yesterday.

by DAVID GIBSON

AFTER seeing over 600 hopefuls in Aberdeen, Kirkcaldy, Inverness, Dundee, Glasgow and Edinburgh, the judges in the Sunday Mail's "Search For Scotland's Tommy Steele"—theatrical impresario and bandleader Bill Paterson and myself—have reached our decision.

Scotland's Tommy Steele is 22-year-old Alex Harvey, of 462 Crown Street, Glasgow, a cooper at the docks.

★★★

Alex put up a wonderful performance at Glasgow's area final. He is a first-rate rock 'n' roll singer (but he's not limited to rock 'n' roll) and his vitality is unlimited.

Bill and I are glad a boy like Alex has won the prizes of £25, a film test and an audition with a recording company, because he's just an ordinary Glasgow lad. In fact, he's not as well-off as many.

Brought up in Kinning Park, he left school early to get to work and bring in some money.

When he was 21, he married his girl friend, a cinema usherette. The only house they could get was a single-end in Crown Street, a cramped little apartment with walls which showed signs of dampness.

Some time ago, Alex bought a smashed-up guitar for £3. He worked on it with loving care and transformed it into a bright, gleaming instrument. With that £3 guitar he sang his way to the top of our contest, competing against guitars which cost anything up to £100.

So, to Alex Harvey, a youngster from the dark back streets of Glasgow, goes this chance to be a star.

If you want to see Scotland's Tommy Steele, for

Alex wins in 57

YOUNG ALEX learned about music during weekend escapes from his dreich and dirty Glasgow life. The solace and silence of the West Highlands was only 90 minutes away (on modern roads it's about 40), so he and his mates would grab guitars and whisky and get lost in the space. They set up home in army surplus tents and picked up songs from army surplus men. The music that made its way across the world to wind up on the banks of Loch Lomond was principally American folk, the stuff that would evolve into C&W.

'It was just an amazing exciting time,' remembers 'General' Jimmy Grimes, a lifelong friend of Alex. 'You would have a fire going, and you had to smoke to keep the midgies away, and it didn't really work so you had to be pissed so as not to go mad. But there was always someone who'd come out the merchant navy or whatever, singing this brilliant new song no one had heard before. Maybe it was because we were doing it so often, but it was dead easy to learn the words, and you'd be singing them all week till you got to learn more songs at the weekend. In those days songs moved from the States to Glasgow then out to the rest of the world.'

Learning the words wasn't enough for Alex, and finally his uncle gave him an old Gibson guitar, which he rebuilt and then learned to play. It must have been an empowering experience – it wasn't like the way 21st century weans learn by playing along to the radio. Alex's journey was infinitely more personal, more organic – these songs were alive; they'd made their way across the planet to speak to *you*, and when you tamed them, you made them your own and learned to speak their language. The power of having a voice to sing and a guitar to play changed Alex's life from very early on.

Of course, he was never remotely like Tommy Steele. In fact, when they met for promotional photos Alex nearly got Tommy arrested. Before becoming the biggest pop star in the country Steele had been in the merchant navy, and on the night he and his Scots counterpart met, his old boat was in Glasgow. The pair went down to the docks, but they were caught as they climbed the fence to get in. This one didn't appear on Alex's criminal record, though – maybe Tommy's people had it hushed up.

Winning the competition was great exposure, giving Alex his first opportunity to tour the circuit – and back then, Scotland had a real variety circuit. Pre-motorway bands toured all the way from Dumfries to Elgin, sometimes spending six or seven hours on backroads to ballrooms. And it wasn't just good for Alex, because several of his friends were able to get on the circuit on the back of their pal's success – after all, in these pre-telly days hardly anyone knew what Scotland's Tommy Steele was meant to look like. One night an Alex impersonator barely escaped with his life when someone brought the Sunday Mail clipping along to the gig and compared likenesses. It can only have been a good time, though, and it was to begin stamping the Alex persona across the country.

His first 'real' musical engagement had been in 1954 as a trumpeter at a friend's wedding. Before that, the legend goes, he'd had 36 jobs, including lion tamer. After the wedding job he played the horn in a few bands for a while, but he was never brilliant at it and really wanted to get serious with guitar and vocals. His first true Harvey-esque incarnation was in the Kansas City Skiffle Group, also known as the Kansas City Counts (yes, he was trying to be rude) playing a rocked-up variant of the American folk he'd started with.

Alex is remembered at this time as a rough-faced character with long hair held by a headband, at a time when the Teddy Boy 'duck's arse' quiff was in. He's also remembered as a wild showman, barely controlled and seriously impressive. The musicians around him didn't like the way he wanted to play, but Alex already had that way about him – he could get you to do what he wanted you to do. Once they joined in, they loved it.

Even at this stage the rising hopeful was sticking it to hapless victims in every direction. Alex and rock'n'roll were close mates because they wanted the same things; but, let there be no doubt, he moved the music to suit his character. As the genre started to become more settled, the jobsworths moved in – older musicians trying to get away with playing different new music the same old way. Acts like that didn't do well against the Harvey machine when it rolled onstage.

Meanwhile, the really clever businessmen tried to stay one step ahead of the game. In the past the entertainments industry had been reasonably stable – but now you had to keep an eye on every act, in case someone was about to hit big and someone else was their management. So it was for Bill Fehilly, one of the two Fehillys who were famous for using the excuse: 'My brother's got the

Left: Alex and
Tommy Steele
meet after the
contest. This
page: Alex promo
pic from the
mid-1960s

money'; he was a step ahead because he loved music. True, he became a millionaire through bingo halls, but he was an impresario too, employing Alex to post bills for him. The two developed a close friendship – in fact, Bill was known as the only man who could control Alex. The relationship was to bear sensational fruit.

With several of his alleged jobs having been at the docks, Alex had strong contacts with sailors and so his access to imported records continued. He and his bands heard people doing things no one this side of the Atlantic had thought of doing. Influenced by the new pop movement, Alex gave up the folk and skiffle and started the Kinning Park Ramblers, named after the area of Glasgow where he was born and grew up.

In 1974 he remembered: 'There were some good clubs in Glasgow at the time, where Maggie Bell started singing with me and my brother Les. We played all kinds of music – everything we could think of – and there was loads of jamming with other musicians. Then at the end of the 50s we heard the black music for the first time. Its influence was very powerful, and I started the Alex Harvey Big Soul Band.'

That entailed binning Alex Harvey and the New Saints, which had replaced the Alex Harvey Band, which had replaced the Ramblers. The thread through it all was, of course, Alex himself, and his energetic, enthralling performances. The Soul Band was to be Alex's biggest success of the 60s and longest-lasting outfit of all time. In many ways it was a prototype for the Sensational Band – it was five times louder and ten times livelier than anything else around.

It's hard to understand now, but this kind of approach was daring for its time. Everyone else played standing still in matching suits, or if they were moving they were doing it in unison. Meanwhile, the Soul Band was going wild on stage. You had them and you had every other band, and if you hadn't heard them or didn't get it, those in the know felt sorry for you. If it was possible to be pop stars in Scotland in the early 60s, Alex and the Soul Band were exactly that.

A big draw in their own right, they bolstered the ticket-shifting power of visiting unknowns like the Beatles, while warming up crowds for folk like Eddie Cochran, Gene Vincent, John Lee Hooker, Acker Bilk, Billy Fury and dozens of other big stars. That great traditionalist George Melly said they had a great feeling for the blues, and they were the first rock band he'd ever enjoyed.

And so it went for three good years – but some of the changes to the circuit weren't as exciting as the rock'n'roll explosion past and the Beatles boom to come. Scotland was stagnating. The variety scene was dying because people began to stay at home and watch television. Many ballrooms had failed to make the change towards pop music, and when they closed down nothing was there to replace them. Staying at home was no longer an option.

So the Soul Band followed the current trend, and left for Germany in 1962. It was the closing years of the beat boom in Hamburg, but there was still plenty of work to be found. It was generally acknowledged that Alex, with eight years of professional musicianship behind him, had a lot more to offer than the cloned Liverpool acts. Towards the end of 63 Polydor recorded the Soul Band Live in the Top Ten Club, only it wasn't the Soul Band and it wasn't live. For contractual reasons it was Kingsize Taylor's backing band, and the 'live' effects, which don't convince the modern listener for a second, were added later.

Alex Harvey and his Soul Band is now regarded as a classic, selling for upward of £70 when it can be found. It features an early version of Framed and I Just Wanna Make Love to You, and most of the tracks demonstrate a mature understanding of the blues genre which other British outfits of the time would have found difficult to match.

Paul Murphy's cover notes, which carefully list Alex's birthday as two years after the event, tell a story that, despite its Sixtiesish language, was oft to be repeated over the next decade:

My first meeting with Alex Harvey was due to a telephone call at 3am on October 13, 1963, to be quite exact (and I always try to be). The manager of one of Hamburg's leading twisteries was on the blower, and informed me at this dreaded hour that I should come to his club immediately and get a load of 'the most fantastic sound since sliced bread'. Although his claim sounded rather stale, it occurred to me that maybe, on this occasion (for there HAD been others) he might possibly be right. So I scrambled into my nitelife clothes, hailed a passing bicycle and headed hotfoot for the Reeperbahn, Hamburg's world-famous Rue de Plaisir.

Upon arriving at the club I was greeted enthusiastically by the manager who hauled me inside, gave me a soft drink with a hard filling and a ringside seat at the twisting turmoil. For about ten minutes I listened to the music whilst secretly memorising the new nifty twisted variations that were being ground out all around me. The band stopped, the twisting stopped... Then Mr Alex Harvey and his Soul band was announced. As all war correspondents say about the beginning of a battle, all hell broke loose (and who says there is NO similarity between the dance floor of a twistery and a battlefield?). I watched and listened completely knocked out by the sheer OOMPH of the Harvey outfit. Indeed, his performance on

The Soul Band and Blues albums

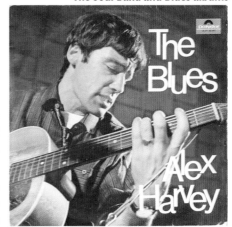

stage has to be seen to be believed. In my mind, I had already signed Harvey after eight minutes of hearing his kind of music. Then came an interval, Harvey came to me, and we both came to an agreement. The result is this LP, recorded on the spot in that nitery.

Interest in all things Hamburg was fading, though, and the album had little effect. Increasingly disillusioned, Alex split the Soul Band in 65 and went back to his blues roots with his 14-year-old brother Les.

Their London-recorded album, The Blues (which is worth more now than the Soul Band album) featured standards such as Waltzing Matilda, Nobody Knows You When You're Down and Out and a stirring St James Infirmary, in which Alex lets out a heart-rending cry of emotional turmoil. There's always been a remarked-upon connection between the west of Scotland and the blues, and Alex demonstrated his grip on the genre once more in an album which had more than one tear-jerking moment. Polydor man David Firmstone, who attended the sessions, later wrote:

A top DJ arrived to interview Alex for his programme, and was so knocked out by what he heard that he sat in the control box for hours before taping the interview. Things took a dramatic turn when Alex sang TB Blues: one of those present collapsed in a paroxysm of grief. It later transpired that his father had died of lung cancer. Indeed, all of us were more than a little overwhelmed by this onslaught of emotions – this, I may say, included the engineers, who are normally quite objective about their work.

The many faces of Alex "Lon Chaney" Harvey... top, the Soul Band (Alex on the left, Bill Patrick on sax and Jimmy Grimes on bass at the right); left, The Blues promo shot; and above, during his psychedelic folk era, on left, with band members

Legend goes that during the session, the producer rejected two tracks and then Polydor boss Horst Schmalzi insisted Alex write a song on the spot. He bowed to the pressure and came up with something, which was rejected after sixteen bars. Despite an outburst of cursing and swearing, Schmalzi demanded another track, and after a short break Alex belted through *Good God Almighty*, defying him to reject it – which, of course, he didn't.

Alex then signed a single deal with Island, who set out to launch him as a bit of a heartthrob. Of particular note is his version of *Agent Double-o Soul*, featuring Stevie Winwood on piano. But as with his previous recorded work, no one was interested and it sank without trace.

Listening to this re-released material now, it's easy to see how one could have loved it or hated it. With a wide range of experience and depth, though, it would be difficult to gain mainstream acceptance; and it says much for the record labels of the time – or little for today's versions – that Polydor were ready to support Alex for a second album.

For the second time in his career he found himself disillusioned, and despite whispers about another Soul Band album he returned to Scotland. He spent 1966 on the famous revolving stage of Glasgow's Dennistoun Palais with ex-Poet George Gallagher, Les, ex-Soul Bandster Bill Patrick and Bill's brother Bobby. The band, which was never named, also featured Isabel Bond as third vocalist.

In 1967 Alex went to try his luck in London. 'I didn't work for nine months and I was about to pack it in,' he recalled, 'then I went to a pub in Soho and bumped into Chas Chandler – I knew him from the Animals. He told me he'd found an amazing new guitarist and took me to see him. It was Jimi Hendrix. He had it all – it was a breath of fresh air! After hearing Hendrix I knew I couldn't pack it in. The next day I was offered a job in a night club.'

Details of the night club job have always been sketchy, but SAHB Fan Michael Barrett recalls his dad Robert throwing a little light on the subject: 'Round about 1967 he was in a wee smoky London pub with some pals. He went out to get some fresh air and saw Alex, dressed in an evening suit and bow tie, eating a hamburger in a phone box. Dad waited till the burger was gone then told Alex he'd been a big fan of the Soul Band, and asked if he was playing anywhere nearby. Alex replied: "I'm playing for the mafia — it ain't really your scene, man..." It sounds like he was trying to earn a crust and had to sing Tony Bennett songs to do it! Of course, when Dad went back into the pub no one believed he'd met Alex.'

Whatever the job was, it led to Alex's employment as guitarist in the pit band of the musical *Hair*. It was more than a show – it was a state of mind (well, a state of head anyway) and all the bright young things were involved: Richard O'Brien, Richard Burton, Tim Curry and many others. During his stint in London Alex became a very weel-kent face indeed.

Ray Conn ran into him by accident about this time, and so began a life-long friendship. 'I'd come out of the merchant navy and with nothing better to do I was heading for the train station to go home to Scotland,' he recalls. 'And I said to the taxi driver, "I've written this song, what do you think I should do with it?" He told me to take it to Tin Pan Alley, so I went there instead of the train station. I ended up in a pub with no toilets, and you had to go round the corner to the public bogs. I waited in the queue until one of the doors swung open and this wee hairy guy staggers out and says: "It's yours – if you want it, pal!" Obviously I got the Scottish accent and he introduced himself as Alex, and later he helped me sell the song.

'He got me a flat in Finsbury Park and used to visit me when I was home from the merchant navy. He used to tell everyone I was an opera singer – I've never even been to an opera! But I think he wrote *Gang Bang* about something we got up to in that flat...'

Alex stayed in the Hair band for four years, and close friends say this was the happiest era of

Alex's life. He enjoyed a relaxing family environment with his second wife Trudy, their son Tyro (he had his elder son, Alex, with first wife Mary), brother Les and close pal Maggie Bell.

Richard O'Brien, who appeared in Hair and later wrote the Rocky Horror Show, recalls Alex the raconteur: 'He was a terrible influence, a cheeky Glasgow chappie. I first spotted him sitting on the bonnet of the truck on the Hair set. He always grabbed that place – he didn't want to be stuck at the back where he couldn't be seen. Another chap came in to redirect the show and pushed him back to join the ranks. We all hated that because we all liked the little smiley person sitting up there watching us perform. Of course, as soon as that director left he was back in his spot again.

'Hair was a big show, a lot of disparate groups of people. There were a lot of people who'd never worked in theatre before and would never do it again, from all walks of life. We just messed about really – nobody really knew what it was about. It wasn't until the movie that someone made sense of the narrative.

'After the show we used to go drinking and he'd make up these wild stories about his time in Europe – at least, I think he was making them up. One never quite knew... He told me he'd picked up the guitar because there was a guy who'd lived opposite him in the Gorbals. "He was an animal," – excuse my Scots accent – "He couldn't play the guitar but he used to put the amplifier in the bath. Oooooh, the noise!" Alex wanted to turn up the volume and make the noise nobody could deny. That's what started him off. But of course, he didn't let the night-job in Hair close all his other musical avenues. He kept himself busy.'

As well as releasing Alex Harvey Sings Songs from Hair, and contributing to the Hair Rave-Up album, he embarked on another more traditional outing with Les: Roman Wall Blues. He joined an experimental band called Rock Workshop, and after the hippy summers of 68 and 69, experimented with psychedelic folk with the short-lived Giant Moth. Yet again, though, personal success was to elude him.

Robert Barrett ran into Alex again around this time. Son Michael remembers: 'Dad was in his local in Glasgow and he heard Alex was playing the Marquee the following night — so he and his pal Jim hitched all the way to London to catch the show. They arrived just as the doors opened and when they got in Alex was sitting at the bar. They told him their story and he was genuinely amazed and happy to hear it. They bought him a few whiskies before he went on but Alex only ever bought them a half-lager each!

'It was pretty much the Hair band that night, but Alex was enthusiastic about a guest trumpeter, Magic Harry Beckett, who was with them. Just before the gig started Jim said, "Give us The Blind Man, Alex". As soon as he went up Alex announced: "This is for two old friends of mine," and played The Blind Man. The Hair Band picked it up straight away — musical genius!

'Dad also remembered a rendition of Honky Tonk Woman which started with the band playing the fanfare from 2001 before the cowbell came in — he said it was the most amazing thing he'd heard in his life.'

Alex was later to say that, while his time in Hair had bored him, it had taught him discipline – all that same thing every night and twice on Saturdays, whether you felt like it or not. Allied with his breadth of musical skill, his years of experience and his personal magnetism, he was a star in waiting – just waiting for that final element to slip into place. And Bill Fehilly came back into his life to provide it.

'POP WEEKLY' AROUND THE SCENE

The persistence of some of Shap's fans! One bird from the backwoods around Norwich smothered "Pop Weekly's" Editorial Desk with so many copies of a letter asking for Helen's unwanted thyroid gland that Ed lost count and started using them to light his cigars with.

Nice work darling, but save the postage to buy another disc with. Let me assure you that EVERY letter sent to "Pop Weekly" is read, and as our local postman does actually deliver them, one's enough.

ALEX HARVEY

Alex Harvey of the lowering dark black looks, which ought to have nailed him up for the feminines to flutter at long ago, cuts a new disc which is a real raver in a bid to crack the soul market right open. 'Tis in fact called *Agent 00 Soul*. In spite of the fact that his "T.Y.L.S." plug featured him in semi-darkness singing outside what appeared to be a jail with a few dustbins outside (presumably for some reason best known to Keith Beckett). *Agent 00 Soul* at the time of writing remains lost in the outer hundreds, no doubt searching for himself . . . but there's time yet. If one can call *00 Soul* a creeper, that is.

'Orrible rumours going around that a whole flush of luvverly female thrushes about to be sponsored in an all out chart bid by several clothing manufacturers. "And in the No. One slot this week we have, by kind permission of Miglethorpe's Better Outerwear, Miss Pebbly Beach singing *Farewell To Moddery, Hail To Toggery*."

On the other hand a number of Glamourcats in sybillant slinky sinny satins on "Top Of The Pops" would really please my old Dad who hasn't thought the scene to be the same since Betty Grable started wearing trousers. Maybe—In the Charts these days you never know.

Saw Gerry Marsden rehearsing for Brian Epstein's Pop Bonanza at the Festival Hall recently. Said he'd cut his new disc that very day, and about time too. Absent from the Charts for many a moon, Gerry, Billy J., Brian P. (well nearly), The Bachelors, Freddie, The Swinging Blue J's and some more, I can't even remember. Do you want 'em back in the charts folks? If you do you'd better do something about it, otherwise it looks as if they've gone for good.

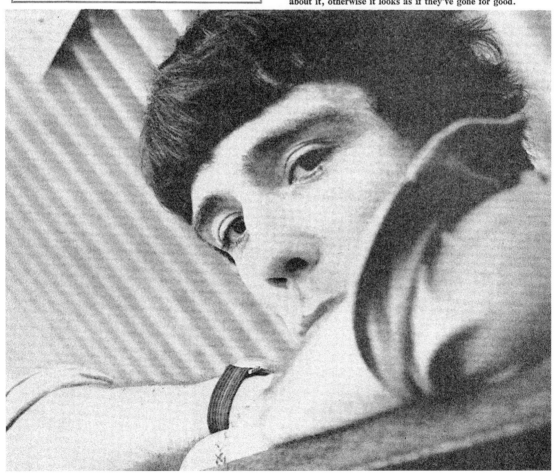

Pop pin-up: Even in the mid-60s Alex's failure to hit big was remarkable in teeny mags like Pop Weekly

2 SUMMER SANDS AND SUMMER DAYS

BY THE MID-60s the first generation of Scots pop stars had spread far from the nation of their birth. Scotland was just too small to hold all that talent, which now asserted itself in London, Hamburg and all stations in between. They'd found their circuit small and boring – but to the next generation, the first folk who'd lived all their lives in the rock'n'roll years, it was a big wide circuit with a million opportunities. People like Alistair Cleminson looked into the distance above their schoolbooks and dreamed of being musicians.

ZAL: I was a self-possessed schoolboy with one eye on my homework and one eye on Chuck Berry or Ray Charles or the wee burds with the heavy eye make-up. All those eyes – it was enough to give you a squint... The music was anything that had rhythm'n'blues or rock'n'roll stamped all over it. There was plenty of Elvis around and Elvis lookalikes roamed the streets giving you the smirk. I thought: one day I'll get a smirk of my own. Eventually the Beatles and the Stones came along and right away you had the perfect excuse to stop dressing like your uncle and singing like Vic Damone. Oh, and of course, there was still the wee burds with the fud-length skirts and grown woman's tits.

I was doubly lucky – first, I got my parents to buy me a Hofner Verithin, a proper electric guitar; and second, I ended up with a girlfriend who had a great pair of grown woman's tits. It was around this time I gave up the notion of playing football every minute of the day and instead spent my time either plagiarising guitar licks or fondling those magnificent tits. What a great name for a band: The Magnificent Tits...

At the age of 15 Alistair discovered the fascinating improvisings of jazz. He heard Wes Montgomery playing guitar and tried to emulate the virtuoso's octaving expressions.

ZAL: It all sounded effortless, and something told me you had to be that good. You had to be serious. To this day I fancy my chances with a bit of fusion – as long as it's in E... Most of the bands at that time were playing the same stuff, but only some were playing all the right chords. It kinda worried me that I might be playing the wrong chords, so I bought a book and picked up a few clues. Call me stubborn or childish and whimsical, but after a while I'd had enough of the book and went back to making shit up. I didn't need to know what fuckin' chord it was as long as it sounded great. I prefer to think of that as defiance rather than stubbornness – defiance infers a sense of dignity is involved. Stubbornness, well, it's just that...

Alistair and next-door neighbour Dave Batchelor had caught the music bug together, and started a band with schoolmates George Gilmour (vocals), Jimmy Brand (drums) and Ricky Archibald (bass). Inspired by the Beatles, Motown, Berry and the vocal groups of the 50s and 60s, Dave brought his six-string skills to balance Alistair's lead guitar. The group called themselves the Bo Weavles and set out for world stardom via every church hall in Scotland, and Dave's mate Eddie Tobin came along for the ride (and the money).

EDDIE: We were 17. Well, Dave was 17 because he's always been six months older than me. Sadly for both us, it'll stop one day... We started in 1964. I remember the drummer didn't have a real kit – he just had a big Salvation Army drum. But we had him, we had two guitars... we had a band! I thought they were fantastic, and I decided there and then I was going to manage the band. I went home and told my mum: we're going to be famous and make money!
DAVE: Naw, that's just what you felt, Eddie – the rest of us were just into the music. We'd have spent the money...
EDDIE: But it wasn't all that difficult to be a band. This Old Heart of Mine was the Scottish national anthem! If you could play that and Please Stay, you were a band.

Dave was later to move to keyboards, inspired by memories of politicians playing classics in his home late at night. His father, active in politics, brought people home at all hours to discuss theories and put the world to rights, and many of the great thinkers were also great players. The energy of one particular socialist thinker crashing out boogie-woogie on the Batchelors' piano led Dave towards the keyboard.

The Bo Weavles became very famous very quickly. Eddie suggests they were Scotland's first boy-band – maybe even Britain's – although obviously they could really play. He encouraged them to maximise on their good looks ('For fuck's sake don't let anyone find out you've got girlfriends!') and dressed them in different-coloured suits. They went to Carnaby Street in London to see the latest fashions for themselves, saw the Move in their musical uniforms and took the idea back to Scotland. In the end they had three or four different costumes, including a set of velvet suits which miraculously appeared soon after the curtains were stolen from the Queen's Hall in Dunoon.

Within a few months, and despite still being at school, they were one of Scotland's Big Four, up there with the Poets, the Pathfinders and the Beatstalkers. In those heady days the Beatstalkers ruled the roost, the Pathfinders led the underground scene and the Poets were untouchable, having been in the charts and everything. Meanwhile the Weavles elbowed their way in somewhere between the Finders and Stalkers, stealing audiences from both to add to their collection of screaming girls.

EDDIE: The Beatstalkers – what a band. The Bo Weavles supported cardboard cutouts of the Stalkers once. I'm serious: they did their set to a sell-out crowd and then the stage turned round and there were these cardboard cutouts of the Beatstalkers and a phone... Then, ring-ring, two thousand people scream like mad, the MC picks up the phone and they hear: Hello, this is Davey... And they go absolutely ballistic! You couldn't believe it – drawing two thousand people to pay to listen to a phone call! How big is that?

Playing gigs like that was a great way to get fans, though. The secret was to remain six months ahead of the competition, by getting hold of imported seven-inches, learning them and performing them long before the other bands heard of them. With their looks, talent and stash of future

Zal through the ages: top, aged 3; middle, at 14 with his sister; above, at 15 with fellow Weavle George Gilmour; left, with his first guitar and his favourite hedge

Ronnie Anderson

The BO-WEAVLES

Sole Management: E.TOBIN
96 Bowfield Crescent,
Glasgow, S.W.2.
Tel: MOS 7552.

FAN CLUBS

GLASGOW   ARGT. PARK
36 — ae Place,
Murray,
East Kilbride.

FIFE and N. SCOTLAND
                PAT ALLISON
78 Denwalk,
Methil, Fife.

Photographed by R. ANDERSON.

The Bo-Weavles: top picture, George, Al (as he signed himself at the time) Dave, Ricky and Jimmy. Left, a promotional postcard shows the band in another set of outfits and advertises their two fan clubs.

Motown hits, they got round the circuit in style, playing as many as nine gigs a week including a double on Fridays and a triple on Saturdays. They took up to £100 a gig when the average wage was £10 or £12 a week – although most of it was swallowed up by the never-ending requirement for equipment. The initial outlay was huge and there was never enough gear.

The band only ever made one record, using a four-track studio in Paisley and borrowing the backing voices of five or six willing girls from the school across the road. It was called Summer Sands, it was recorded under the auspices of Rolling Stones manager Tony Calder, and it's reputed to be the worst-ever single in world music history. But the novelty and excitement of having cut a record dwarfed any criticism of the mere content, and dreams of American tours ended the Weavles' heads. As Eddie notes, one of the best things about being young is everything's amazing. Meanwhile, America or no, the Bo Weavles were having a good time.

EDDIE: You could shag yourself to death.
DAVE: No, no – you could play music close to your heart. And then shag yourself to death.
EDDIE: Except in Portpatrick, where all the birds vanished as soon as the show was over. It was like something out of the X Files: we came out of the hall and there was nothing but wind and water...

BACK in the industrial backwaters of Coatbridge, two cousins were steering a parallel course with the Weavles from Penilee. Hugh McKenna came from a true showbiz background. His mother had been a variety-hall singer, and her mother and father had been a leading female vocalist and big-name comedian respectively. Hugh's father had been given an accordion at the age of 14 and turned it into a lifelong career in music, making a living out of busking in his younger years, until summer seasons and big shows took over his life; then when Hugh was young he'd seen the variety scene start to collapse under the onslaught of television. He saw the writing on the wall and got out — but not before Hugh had become his co-star.

HUGH: When I was 5 my parents had a summer season in Perth, and the landlord of our digs gave me a mouth-organ. By the end of the day I'd learned to play two tunes on it – Scotland The Brave and a little jig – and I could do them both from beginning to end. My parents were overjoyed! So my father got me to come on stage with him and play a Scottish reel along with his piano. The problem was, you can't change the key of a mouth-organ. He started playing in G and I could only play in C, so I had to stop the show and tell him: 'Dada, you're in the wrong key!' Everyone thought it was part of the act...

Surrounded by music as he was, Hugh began learning the piano aged 7 (eventually achieving Grade 8) and by 13 or 14 he could work out and play a wide range of jazz standards. He was inspired by Gerschwin, Porter and Berlin, and loved standards like Night and Day, In The Mood For Love and Fly Me to the Moon. He'd also developed a feel for the twelve-bar blues. And so had his cousin Eddie.

TED: I used to go and see Hugh every Sunday, taking the Co-operative money to his mum. My mother played piano but my father wasn't musical, although he appreciated music. I was into Astaire and Rogers and didn't want to go to the Cubs because of that, then my Uncle Paddy took me into a wee room and played me Jailhouse Rock – 'There ye are, son, that's rock'n'roll!' I thought it was great. So I got into rhythm, my dad made my first sticks out of dowling rods, and I began

Above: Rare Breed (Hugh, Tom, Eddie, Jim, Owen); below: Bubbles (Hugh, Owen, Tom, Eddie and Jim in front)

playing along to my records on the ironing board. So Hugh and I started getting closer through the music, which was something that wasn't happening otherwise.

The McKenna cousins' Sunday afternoon music club started after Hugh came back from football and then did his piano practice. Then they'd get out the snare drum Hugh's father owned, which had a hole in the top skin so had to played upside down. This wasn't a big problem to Eddie, who was blown away with the excitement of hitting a real drum. They carried on until Eddie was given his first kit by his father, and then Hugh did the travelling. The loudest noise was Hugh's foot on the piano pedals, a thumping matched by the downstairs neighbour thumping back up in frustration. Meanwhile, though, the veranda doors were open and the local kids enjoyed the entertainment. It was nearly like playing a gig.

They began rehearsing at school until they met Owen Mullen and Jim Coventry who played their own gigs. One night they were on at Bellshill so Eddie and Hugh went to see them, and ended up sitting in on a wee set before the main act came on. The schoolboy performance was well-received, and the Vibrations were born. It was a difficult birth.

Hugh's dad wouldn't buy him a keyboard, despite Eddie's best efforts at persuasion, so he wasn't able to join. Things started looking up when they secured a support slot with the Poets at Coatbridge Town Hall, with a lineup including guitarist Arthur McWilliams (who was once in the Graduates with McKenna schoolmate John Reid, the government minister).

TED: I was chuffed: we're in a band, it's starting to happen! The first band went on and their guitarist starting churning it out, and Arthur looked at him, picked up his guitar and went home. I had to get a lift to his house and drag him back, while he kept saying, 'I canny dae it!' Shortly after that he just jacked it. I was suicidal because our band was splitting up... Really suicidal. I'd sit on the school bus contemplating really dark things...

Then Hugh was invited to audition for a band called the Rare Breed, which had its own gear. Eddie went along and there was a drumkit in the audition room, so he started playing along with Hugh, and the rare Breed sacked their drummer to get him on board.

TED: Eddie Tobin was the agent, you see the connection? So there must have been money around... There was – I always had money in my pocket because I didn't drink or smoke like the others. Anyway, the bass player kept saying he couldn't rehearse because his girlfriend wanted to go to the pictures or whatever, and we were like, 'Aye, right', and then one night he said he couldn't do a gig because he was going out with her, so we forced him to do the gig then fired him, and I got Owen in. Then I was thinking, could we do a Sam and Dave thing? So we got Jim in too, and then the other singer jacked it because Jim was better... Suddenly Tom Wigfield was the only one left, and we'd taken over Rare Breed – only just and only fair!

The McKennas were off, round the circuit like their future bandmates. They took as many support slots as they could get, honing their skills, then living through excruciating trips home with their grumpy manager stroke roadie stroke plasterer (that was his day job).

TED: If Sandy was in a bad mood he'd drive us all the way home from places like Dunoon without a chippie stop or anything! So we ended up getting our own van and looking after our own affairs. We were doing not bad on our own – we weren't as big as some of the bands but we had our own fan base. I'd never had a job but the other guys had jacked theirs in. To mark our going pro we changed the name of the band to Bubbles. I'll never know why we did that – stupid name! I think it was because we were a pop band. Get it? But we were getting around, playing everywhere and anywhere, and our big thing was we did the Radio One Club a couple of times and got broadcast on the radio.

Hugh suggests they had to change their name after someone vandalised a poster, replacing 'Rare Breed' with 'Pan Breed' and thus rendering the Scots rhyming slang for 'deid' (dead).

The formula remained as it had always been: Bubbles churned out the music of the Beatles, the Kinks, the Hollies and Motown. They had one original track, Summer Days, which Hugh wrote. The big difference was they no longer faced the prospect of gigging all weekend, getting home at 4am and having to get up for school a few hours later. After supporting the Bo Weavles they kitted themselves out with matching suits. And they rehearsed like fuck.

HUGH: There was a circuit, town halls, youth clubs, church halls – a real circuit. We were quite professional about it. We'd rehearse five times a week. Most days we went in about 12, had

Bubbles at Kilmarnock Grand Hall (honest)

something to eat, then worked through until 5. We were serious – but we didn't take it too seriously. Mind you, we really wanted to sound good. We liked doing gigs for dancing – there were girls about and we enjoyed that as well. But we never went overboard with the social side of things. It was the fun of getting onstage and playing all these songs, sounding like the records, people liking it. There was a buzz. They hadn't heard the acts that recorded these tracks so they'd hear us playing what they heard on the radio: a live band.

But it was very quiet amplification... I remember John Reid's Graduates was the first band I ever heard. They had 30 watt amps and I'd never heard anything so loud in my life! It blew me out the room! Nowadays 30,000 watts wouldn't blow me out the room.

Although the Scottish circuit was still relatively vibrant, one wouldn't want to stay there for ever. Brian Hogg, writer of the History of Scottish Rock and Pop, remembers a situation familiar to Alex's generation, and even today's young talent. 'It was the age-old problem of being too far away from the action,' he says. 'It was imperative to make a move – maybe not to Hamburg any more, but definitely London. But it wasn't an easy thing to do.

'The Poets, for example, were not only one of the best bands in Scotland, but one of the best bands *ever* – but it was purely good fortune that the Stones' manager, Andrew Loog Oldham, found them and took them to London. Dean Ford and the Gaylords, later the Marmalade, knew they'd been doing well here but would have to make it in London, and they did. Whereas the Beatstalkers, who were arguably more popular in Glasgow, couldn't make it at all down south.'

Failure to achieve a southward motion meant all was not well inside the Bubbles; and the McKennas went their separate ways when the Dream Police poached Eddie. In a twist of fate he'd had a word with his band before a show, telling them he was getting bored. That evening he saw Hamish and Joe from the Police beside the stage, and he knew straight away they were there to ask him to join. Sure enough, they did. After a night of sitting up with Hugh, listening to Radio Luxembourg

Ronnie Anderson

Zal prepares for a
Bo Weavles show
near the end of the
band's career

and talking about everything, he made his decision and headed south to join a London-based band that had recorded an album and been on tour in Europe.

TED: All the guys said: 'Come on, it's a big step up – you've got to do it'. So I did. I went down to London and moved in to the Marmalade's flat, where the Dream Police lived. The first night I was there we went out for a drink and George Harrison was in the pub. They bought me a new drumkit, and Dougie Henderson from the Marmalade came with me to choose cymbals – we went to the Arbiter warehouse and I got to pick them from stacks and stacks. I got Dougie to play the ones I liked till I'd chosen. Then the first gig I did was with the Groundhogs in Swansea. I thought, this is the place to be.

HUGH: I'd been getting bored with Bubbles too, so I told Eddie, do this, it'll be good for you. And so that was him in the Dream Police. Then I changed my mind about quitting Bubbles, but a few weeks later on we had an argument and I went ahead and left. I didn't have anywhere else to go. That was the only time in my career when my parents said to me: 'Are you sure you know what you're doing?' But with the arrogance of youth I thought, something will come along. And it did, actually.

MONTH. JANUARY.				ACT. BUBBLES.	
DATE.	VENUE.	TIMES.	FEE.	SPOTS.	REMARKS.
1.	FRI. KINEMA DUNFERMLINE	8–1	30.	1 HOUR.	(CASH)
2.	SAT KENFREW Y.M.	8–11³⁰	35	2 × 45.	(CASH)
3.	SUN CUMNOCK TOWN HALL	10–2	35?	2 × 45.	(CASH)
4.					
5.					
6.	WED ST ALOYSUS CHURCH HALL	8–11	25.		
7.					
8.	FRI. KAD1/KILMARNOCK	9–1	30+35	2 × 45	(BOTH CHEQUE)
9.	SAT FLAMINGO GLASGOW	7³⁰–11	40.	—	(CASH)
10.	SUN				
11.	MON CRAGBURN GOUROCK.	7³⁰–11³⁰	25.	—	(CHEQUE)
12.					
13.					
14.	THU ANGUS HOTEL DUNDEE	9–1	40	2 × 45?	(CASH)
15.	FRI. ABERDEEN		50		(CASH)
16.	SAT ABERDEEN.		50.		(CASH)
17.	SUN ABERDEEN.		50.		(CASH)
18.					
19.					
20.					
21.	THU NEWMAINS C.C.	7³⁰–11	20.		(CASH)
22.	FRI. ELECTRIC GARDENS.		30		(CASH)
23.	SAT ELECTRIC GARDENS.		35		(CASH)
24.	SUN ST. PATS. COATBRIDGE	8–11	35		(CASH)
25.					
26.					
27.					
28.	THU TROCADERO HAMILTON		15		(CASH)
29.	FRI. KINEMA. DUNFERMLINE		30		(CASH)
30.	SAT STRATHCLYDE U/O.	8–1	40		(CHEQUE)
31.	SUN ST ANTHONYS GOVAN		25		(CASH).

A Bubbles monthly schedule shows how busy the Scottish circuit was at the end of the 1960s

Hugh landed in a band with Davie Nicholson and Hugh Nicholson, managed by their big brother Matt Nicholson. They called the band Nicholson. Along with drummer Nod Kelly they had a moderately successful wee time of it. Hugh began writing and came up with three or four songs, which he regarded as only tinkering about. One of the tracks, Oh Carol, was used as the B-side when the band had a Decca tryout — but Hugh lost the acetate in the pub, although he remembers the song fondly.

As the 60s drew to a close, the rock'n'roll scene began to enter another transition phase. Woodstock and the hippie movement was changing the course of youth culture. Power trios and prog rock outfits heralded the advent of the virtuoso rock star. And while a disillusioned Alex Harvey was being re-inspired by Hendrix, the Bo Weavles were getting a creative kick in the stones from similar quarters.

SUPERGROUP 3

IT WASN'T JUST THE WINNERS who won the Second World War. Even the world's most-bombed rose again to become giants of globalisation. The new mix had less space for the British stiff upper lip of optimism, tinted with colours of fresh beginnings. Instead Vietnam brought a nastier type of peace and love, an unhappy aggressive love that bordered on refusal to accept the human condition. In the world of rock'n'roll, people didn't want to wear uniforms and sing about summer any more. They knew they were poor.

It was the arse-end of the ballroom days, but the scene was still vibrant. A good night was about how busy the hall was – which is to say, how many girls were in. You paid 10s to see a band if they were sexy enough to pull the burds in; then in second place you considered their talent and stage act. Chris McClure and the early Bay City Rollers were putting on some of the best shows in town. Dance halls heaved with sexual excitement and physical danger.

You arrived at a pub near the venue and had a few drinks until it shut at 10pm, then moved to the no-alcohol-served hall as it opened for the evening. You took stock of the support band, considering whether to approve, trying to be pretty vocal about your decision. You waited for the main act to come on and moved up to the front, scanning for the best gear, the best lights, the best outfits, the best girls.

Then the show, and usually the barney, kicked off. You had to watch yourself because you got chucked out for anything – anything. The bouncers took no prisoners, and it was a real and regular scunner to be ejected without seeing the band you came for, wasting all that money while your pals lived it up. For better or worse you'd end up outside the hall just around the end of the night, waiting for the chance to pull anyone you'd either already got off with or fancied a go at. If you'd somehow been separated from your pals, or it was a particularly violent evening, single girls would try to make themselves available to you: the not-often-broken rule being that a bloke with a bird was exempt from a kicking. A friendly girl was your ticket to the bus or taxi in safety. Try to make sure your suit survives the night intact, and see you all next week.

But these days were passing. Disco was coming in and live music was becoming something you sat down at rather than danced to. It was all prog rock's fault. Well, and television's.

The new, smaller scene consisted of outfits like the Verge, Agatha's Moment and HiFi Combo – the latter being the only band in the world that went to the butcher before every gig. They'd buy a bag of offal and place it in a coffin with their singer, then carry it to the centre of the stage. Covered in flour, they'd begin their show as the singer stood up, pulled the entrails out of his shirt and threw them into the audience. Which was alright if you happened to be hungry and had a portable barbecue with you.

But this was where it was at, and a good deal of the paying punterage voted for disco. Those who were staying on the scene wanted to stay still during the show; they wanted all senses entertained by the guys up front, and weren't going to do half your job for you by dancing. The best bands on the scene were beginning to embrace theatrical shows. The rest were becoming pub rock bands.

CHRIS GLEN was of the opinion that was most bands were fuckin' mingin'. He got himself round the circuit and spent a lot of time naked; he made his own clothes and they were so much better than his mates' they borrowed them to wear on stage. And as he waited in the dressing room for his gear to come back, he'd listen to the shows – even big-name act performances – and think:

CHRIS: I can do better than that and I can't even play! So I borrowed a bass and tinkered for a while, and decided I was into it. I sold my scooter to put the money towards a bass, my dad signed the credit deal in McCormack's, and I ended up with two Vox Foundations, a Vox 100 watt and a Gibson EBO bass. Thing was, because of my size it was like a banjo on me, so I immediately traded it in for the Fender – the one I've still got.

Then I started Jade with a few mates from Pollokshields. We got a wee carrot-heided guy called Jim Diamond to sing for us – and he ended up becoming Jim Diamond. And then Eddie Tobin approached me about joining Mustard. But I wasn't into it because they'd been the Bo Weavles, and that had been a harmony band. Eddie told me, it's okay, we're going to become Tear Gas...

ZAL: Mustard was our big transition. Woodstock had been part of it – people decided they weren't going to be tainted with the word 'pop' any more. They wanted to be seen as progressive.

Everybody started aspiring to the big names that had come to the fore as exponents of their instruments. Everyone was trying to be virtuoso, whereas before that everyone had been playing as a backing group from the soul era. Now we had driving forces – your Jimmy Pages, Hendrixes, Claptons... It was a really big change. It wasn't like the Beatles any more. We'd all moved on.

Tel: DOUglas 1830

STATEMENT

366

69a WEST REGENT STREET

Glasgow, C.2. 15. 1. 70 19

M r. C. McKenna

BRADLEYS (MUSIC) LTD.

MUSICAL INSTRUMENTS

	Balance.	£27.	18	6
Eddie				
Something more to				
account please				

Ted in the red in 1970

The lineup changed with the name and the music: Andy Mulvey came in from the Poets to sing, and Gil Lavis (later to join Squeeze and currently in Jools Holland's band) became the drummer. Meanwhile a character by the name of Dashing Dick Darleson (from Dawlish in Devon) played bass for a short while. It was a very unhappy lineup.

TED: Bubbles supported that lineup at the Electric Gardens. I'd been talking to Gil before he went on and I was really into what he was saying – he was a real drummer's drummer. But now Andy was shouting at him on the stage. Gil was taking pelters off the singer... Then when they came off Andy punched him.

DAVE: We were very cruel to Gil. He wore a Dr Kildare-type collar with a button on the side and a silver lame suit, and played like Buddy Rich with a big smile. But it was wrong for us. Andy used to scream at him to play louder, hit the things, and his hands were so blistered he had to wear gloves.

CHRIS: Gil's favourite trick was he could do a shite without using toilet paper – he'd stand up above the pan, pull the cheeks of his arse apart and fire a shite out, then run a bit of toilet paper through to prove there were no marks on it.

TED: He saved a fortune...

Eddie Tobin recalls the night Andy punched Gil was the night he knew he wanted Ted in the band; but Wullie Monroe from Ritchie Blackmore's Mandrake Root was next on the drum stool. He's remembered as a wonderful wee guy, but mental. Clad in a black holocaust cloak, round glasses and a wide-brimmed hat, his half-Terry-Pratchet, half-Harry-Potter look matched the confusion of his social presence. After seeing 2001: A Space Odyssey, he built himself a Tycho Monolith and placed it in his room, which had been painted black. Including the windows. Wullie clearly shared thoughts with Blackmore – no one else knew what they were, but they shared them. Nevertheless, he was a stunning addition to the band:

DAVE: The first time we saw him we were impressed. He was a bit like Ginger Baker, with a real rolling style and big heavy rock galloping.

EDDIE: He was like Animal from the Muppets. A very bizarre person – he'd take any drugs in any orifice. He was a nice drummer to watch, though. There was a very visual aspect to his playing.

Eddie also maintains the only reason he asked Chris to join the band was because he owned a six-wheel transit van. This was more than minutiae: his bass playing wasn't in doubt but the van made him essential to the plot. There was something awe-inspiring about these vehicles, with their stickers and their scratches. You'd arrived – you were in a higher league than the poor souls with short-wheelbase transits. And the more beaten-up looking it was, the longer it had been on the road, the more rock it was. And it had to be primer grey too, so it looked the part when it was parked outside McCormack's music shop.

The huge changes on the scene were making people take stock of more than just the music they wanted to play. Andy Mulvey decided to set out for a new life in Africa, and so Dave Lennox was lined up as his replacement. But just before a tour of Germany, Dave pulled out at the last minute; and, jammed in panic-mode, the only solution for the newly-named Tear Gas was for Dave Batchelor to take over the mike, and ex-Beatstalker Eddie Campbell to come in on keyboards.

DAVE: I was in at the deep end. It was all a blur. I can't remember any of it at all, except that the gigs were fantastic.

EDDIE: Dave didn't get a lot of say in it – he was the only option. We looked round the band and pointed the finger, and that was it. Fortunately, he was brilliant! And fortunately, dope was coming in then so everyone was happy and everything was calm...

From the outset Tear Gas were on a mission to be the loudest, hardest, riffiest band in the country. Clad in their not-a-uniform-but-still-trademark outfits (leather, Afghan coats, ripped jeans, Beatle-boots) they gallivanted across the prog rock circuit giving it utter utter laldy. The first song they performed together was Born To Be Wild, a sensational rip-roaring opener, the effect of which was slightly dented by Wullie slamming his bass pedal right through the drumskin, requiring a pause-and-reset after 4.08 bars of the band's career ('Here we are... Tear Gas! Oh,

Piggy-era Tear Gas: above, Dave, Eddie, Wullie, Zal, Chris. Below: the comic-book influence on the album sleeve

fuck... Start again...'). Meanwhile, Eddie Campbell would treat the punters to his Jimi Hendrix impersonation during Purple Haze, taking his false teeth out and playing guitar with them.

The transition was nearly complete. Mustard was Tear Gas and the lineup was Batchelor (vocals), Cleminson (guitar), Glen (bass), Campbell (keyboards), Monroe (drums) and Tobin (management). The matching-suit look had gone through an interim shirt'n'tie phase and wound up in the long-hair look. The harmonic pop had been dumped in favour of progressive rock. The smiley-smiley row of glittery crooners were now a shoe-gazy assemblage of cutting-edge artists. The optimistic schoolboys were battle-hardened rock musicians, aware that life was shite. It was time for the band to leave their parents' homes and go pro. And it was time for Al to become Zal.

ZAL: Going pro meant leaving your job and signing on. I didn't have a job – I sat my Highers, jumped on the train, went to Aberdeen for a gig, and that was me. Davie worked in an architect's office and Chris was a quantity surveyor – he still talks about his theodolite with relish. It was big decision, but it was like, you have to jack it in because there isn't time to play, rehearse and get to gigs and still be home in time to get up for a job. And Eddie would push us on, saying, you need to be pro. And you'd look over your shoulders at other bands who were getting more gigs, going further by being more pro. It takes on a little more attitude. Your parents look more askance when they realise you're not going to get a job. I was on the dole when I married Sandra. But the only really big difference between amateur and pro was that we now rehearsed instead of practicing...

We couldn't live at home any more, so the band took a flat in Battlefield. It was now a proper, progressive rock group, loud as fuck and hairy as coconuts. By this time I'd been renamed Zal – I think Dave came up with it, maybe because of the Lovin' Spoonful guy. But I liked it – it had an unusual sound. No one knew if you were from Manchester or Mars, or better still, a Hungarian dissident whose family had joined a circus to escape the troubles. I became Zal.

TED: I became Ted about then too. I'd always been Eddie – although come to think of it there were enough Eddies around. Then we were in Arran, playing football with Midge Ure's Slik, except they were called Salvation; I got the ball and someone went, 'Haw, big Ted's got it!' And the whole music fraternity just went with it...

ZAL: Not quite as good as 'Zal', though.

TED[singing]: Zal kills germs, just kicks them out
             Zal's the thing to pine about
             For that zingy zingy scent of pine
             Zal disinfects it every time!

ZAL: Aye... Then there's Izal toilet paper, that horrible shiny tracing paper you got in the public baths. It didn't absorb anything - it just spread the shit all over your arse and you had to make a crisp-poke shape and scoop... I, Zal...

TED: I think I had an easier time with my name.

THEY BECAME the rock giants of Scotland, and in some circles became known as Fear Gas because of their sheer volume. Eddie took the recently made-it Nazareth to see the band in Strathclyde University, but despite the Fife rockers owning a huge WEM sound system, they couldn't believe the noise level Tear Gas attained.

They supported Deep Purple at a time when they were a moderately successful rock group, the size of Slade or Status Quo; and they recall the evening they heard Black Night for the first time and knew Purple were about to be huge. They lived through Marc Bolan's Tyrannosaurus Rex era, when the future glam god inscribed a circle on the floor and sat down in it to play. In the Electric Gardens he did it so far back on the large stage the seated audience couldn't see him, prompting a very polite heckle: 'Excuse me Mister Bolan! Can you draw yer circle at the front o'the stage please?'

Life consisted of constant concerting, and a drinking marathon every dole day – certainly for those members who lived in the band's flat – involving Tornado tonic wine mixed with Scrumpy from the infamous Saracen's Head ('Sarry Heid') pub. Chris' six-wheel transit rolled from venue to venue with Eddie Campbell's giant Hammond B3 on the roof-rack, attracting the attention of the authorities from time to time. In one instance, roadie John was accused of drunk driving, the constable's justification being: 'You're staggering'. 'You're not too bad yourself,' replied John as the handcuffs came out.

Tear Gas acquired a reputation for mooning, in one famous incident spending 40 minutes stuck in traffic in Edinburgh's Princes Street, taking turns to ensure there was always an arse in the van's window. During a fire alarm at Jonesy's in Ayr, the 600 fans waiting outside for the all-clear were treated to a ringside view of the Cleminson rear from the window above the main entrance. Among the viewers was the club's regional manager, who banned the band from ever returning.

While it was the ambition of every pop group to cut a single, rock bands aimed for recording an album, and in 1970 Tear Gas headed to London to do just that. Piggy Go Getter was created in a pokey basement while the band stayed together in one room at the Grantleigh Hotel. The general feeling is it doesn't stand the test of time too well – and it didn't even then; but one's first album will always hold a special place in one's heart.

Scotland's supergroup?

Glasgow group, Teargas, could almost be termed a Scottish supergroup. The line-up includes names from four of the big groups in the country. Vocalist Dave Batchelor comes from the late lamented Bo Weavils, likewise lead guitarist Zal Cleminson. Drummer Willie Munroe came from Rite-Tyme, organist Eddie Campbell from the Beatstalkers and bass guitarist Chris Glen from Jade.

They have been together as Teargas for seven months, during which time, they have written a vast amount of material between them. They have completed fourteen numbers which they would like to record for an album, but want to find a really striking number for a single first.

They do heavy rock and roll numbers, a commercial version of Led Zeppelin. They are also absolutely insane. To prove the point, they were on the road to Peebles recently, but were getting a little bored in the van. To relive the monotony, they drove the van into a farm, astounding the farmer and his wife, and set up the equipment in the biggest farm, insisting that it was Peebles' Town Hall.

Should you wish to actually witness this mob at work, here are their diary dates for near future.

November 14th the Cragburn, Gourock; 15th Olympia, East Kilbride; 19th Electric Garden, Glasgow; 22nd Beach Pavilion, Girvan; 23rd Newtongrange; and 24th Town Hall, Port Glasgow.

CHRIS: It was done on a double-four-track studio. We had to do four tracks then bounce them onto the other four-track, so you had to mix as you were going. You really had to think ahead because once you committed it that was it. It didn't sound that bad for the time, but because it was done on a tight schedule and to a strict budget it was very weak to me. It sounded very compressed, not like us at all.

DAVE: The producer, Tony Chapman, was into the Band and that kind of stuff, and the album came out with that kind of energy, flat and boxy, whereas we were nothing like that. But we were naïve.

ZAL: There's some good hard riffs going on, but it's done in a running-through-the-fields airy-fairy Mamas-and-Papas way. It was the production that made it not happen. At the time I was chuffed to bits at doing it at all – you think, you've made a record, so that's the best you can do. I wrote a song, it got recorded, fantastic. Later on you think, ouch! But there's a great kind of naïve charm to it – the music has a texture you could use today. But the thing was, it wasn't up to you whether you'd played well or not. The producer decided how good you'd been. You didn't get the chance to say, I like that take, or, let's do it again. He decided and that was the end of it.

TED: I was surprised by the album – I didn't think it was anything like the band I heard.

Piggy Go Getter only sold a few thousand copies, and if you've got one today you're minted. The relative dissatisfaction with the end result led to lineup changes. Eddie Campbell headed for pastures new, which, on the bright side, meant no more lugging the Hammond up to his high-rise flat at Moss Heights. Then Wullie moved on in a manner that left the Dream Police reeling.

TED: I'd been in London for about six months and we'd done a bit of recording. Then one day I was suddenly told that Hamish had quit, and he'd taken Wullie from Tear Gas and they were starting a new band. Hamish didn't say anything, he just walked out – actually I'll need to see him about that... So I knew Tear Gas needed a drummer, and I phoned Eddie and told him I'd be right up. The next day I was heading back to Glasgow.

They were a band that had an album behind them and they were very different from the other bands around – for a start they did their own tracks. They had a style and a sound about them. They'd gone from being the teenybopper boys to being the bad boys – they had a dangerous image, while we were all still poppy. That appealed to me. I've always liked a bit of danger in my music. My first impression was, who's this big posin' bastard Glen? He was at it with me from the start...

CHRIS: Ted arriving was a major change for us. It was a big thing. I'd only seen him in Bubbles, doing covers, no originals, playing and singing harmonies and all that... he looked pretty straight compared to the animal we'd had before. Ted was all nicey-nicey and Wullie came out with the big rock gallops... So I went up to him on the first day and said:

    CHRIS: Can you do a gallop?

    TED: What do you mean, a gallop?

    CHRIS: Well, a diddly–rumpity... you know...

    TED: What, like this? [plays ferocious big fuckin' monster riff]

    CHRIS [to band]: He'll do for me.

For just about the first time since the beginning, the band was without a keyboard player, and this was the lineup that recorded the second album, Tear Gas, in 1971. Again, Stones manager Tony Calder was behind the scenes, showing a lot of interest in the band and bringing big names into play for them. Two London studios were used this time: an eight-track room at London Weekend Television and a sixteen-track setup at Island Studios, Basing Street.

It was a difficult time for Ted. It was his first album experience, and as the engineer adjusted the drum setup he realised it was being ruined.

TED: It was a traumatic experience. London Weekend was a huge dead room, terrible for ambient drums. But on top of that, Tony and his engineer took the front head off my bass drum, took the bottom heads off my toms, put tape all over the heads – and it didn't sound like me. My drums were always open and ambient, the way Bonham sounded, but these guys had other ideas and I was just choked. It made me overplay to try and get some life out of them. It ruined my playing and I didn't think it was anything like my best work. When we moved to Basing Street they set the drums up right, but by that time I was so tense and nervous about the whole thing I overplayed again – and I kept making mistakes. If you listen to Tear Gas you can hear all those mistakes, just from the sheer mental mayhem in my head. I remember going onto the roof and thinking, I can't play any more. But... All things considered it was an interesting album, and it stands up today.

If it had been hard for Ted, it was tortuous for Dave, who by now had realised he was out of his depth on vocals.

DAVE: Both albums were very strange for me. I know it's a cliché, but it just freaked me hearing my own voice back. I was terrified. I couldn't get inside the song because I was hearing this voice coming back and it didn't sound like me. I'd just become a singer – a brand new job to learn, and I was trying to sing like Stevie Winwood, Sam and Dave, people like that. I knew something was wrong but it was only years later I realised that stuff didn't work with my voice, and I shouldn't have been trying it. Hamish came in to do backing vocals and there was an outro that needed a bit of vocal work, and he was telling me, try it, let yourself go. And I just could not do it. It wasn't a pleasant experience at all. I can listen to it now and find a lot of pluses, but not then. In my naïveté I was blown away by the Tony Calder big business connection, and the brilliant album cover by Hipgnosis, who did the Pink Floyd stuff.

CHRIS: We did Jailhouse Rock and All Shook Up in Basing Street. It was called a live version but the truth was we only had the studio for a day and there wasn't time for overdubs — so we had to do it that way. We did play those songs very well. I don't know how well it works on the album but we did them brilliantly. It was really great fun and I enjoyed every minute. I can honestly tell you I don't hear the album when I play it – I remember the way we used to play those songs live, and it was amazing. A very good album. We never got any money for it, of course, as was the way of all things...

TED: Where is My Answer is a good one, a slow one. It sounded like Dave had drunk a bottle of Benylin before he sang it, it's so soft and easy. It was so quiet we got the benefit of the studio's sound quality. There's a lot of things on that album that are really really good. When I forget what I don't like about the drums I can enjoy it. Piggy had sounded too nice. Wullie was the best drummer in Scotland in my book, although he used to hate me doing all the rudiments because I knew that shit and he wasn't that disciplined... But he had great riffs, and then on Piggy he'd sounded too nice. Very disappointing.

EDDIE: The first album didn't represent the band at all... but the second one was there, it was them, and I mean that as someone who knew them onstage and offstage. I think Jailhouse Rock is a sensational track for today – it would make a great single. I wish someone would release it...

ZAL: The two Tear Gas albums are like opposite ends of a very bad perm. The first one starts off in the basin, with lots of hot water, shampoo and fanciful patter. The second is when you emerge from the drier and stare, catatonic, into the mirror.

TEAR GAS did a lot better than Piggy Go Getter and it carried the band onward, if not quite upward. Perhaps the Fear Gas reputation did as much harm as good. Zal and Chris were using 200 watt amps they'd had modded up to 250 watts, using two and four cabinets respectively – which was a huge huge sound back then. After a double-header with Berserk Crocodile, Hamish and Wullie's new band, Hamish told them: 'Here, boys, that's just out o'order – ye just canny play that loud...'

In any respect, the absence of keyboard was an issue. Zal realised later that because his style was an undisciplined mishmash of rhythm and lead, he needed the structure provided by the keys; at the time he just wanted them because he liked them. Meanwhile, Ted felt the music needed another dimension, and so for the second time he pushed Hugh into the situation.

HUGH: I wasn't really into heavy rock at all, not even Zeppelin and people that size. I'd done Who stuff, but that was about it. I liked a lot of singer-songwriters at the time. I didn't have a record collection – I had to like something a lot to actually buy it, and anyway I didn't have any money. But I thought Elton John's first album was very good and I liked Joni Mitchell a lot. Yes was the first album I bought. Having been through SAHB I think I'd like Tear Gas a lot more now than I did then.

It was the end of the road for Dave's vocal career, because Hugh took over that role as well. In some ways it was a relief for Dave, who set about taking over some management chores and also becoming the band's sound man, putting himself on a second steep learning curve for Tear Gas. It

Ronnie Anderson

Dave pictured around the time he became Tear Gas' singer

Ted, Zal, Chris and Dave at Tear Gas time

can only have been an uncomfortable situation - although Eddie points out since there wasn't any money in the band it wasn't as big a deal as it could have been.

ZAL: It was a very odd political moment – I cannot see how that all brought itself about, who made those decisions. We must have talked around it for a long time, but someone must have made an executive decision. Probably Eddie, which would have been weird because they were best mates. I think I was very subservient at that time, I just went with the flow. It all had a democratic feel. I think Dave himself had made the odd comment about not feeling right anyway – we were looking for a Robert Plant, but Dave wasn't that. He's a good looking guy, he definitely had the look, but it just wasn't coming across and projecting. The thing is, it's all very well being mates and everyone getting along, but you become too subjective about it and that's why a lot of people don't get anywhere.

DAVE: It was a continuation of the team. I didn't know much but I knew what we should sound like so it was just a matter of getting there. I was used to being in at the deep end by now, so I got there quite quickly!

TED: We were always very aware of the fact that generating a good sound was an important part of moving an audience. And the louder you are – and no one was louder than us – the more important it becomes. The confidence of knowing we sounded great out front made a big difference.

The difference was clear to audiences all over the country, who revelled in the band's shock factor while, hopefully, getting into the musical expression too. The rocky road was long, never-ending, and countless hours in cooped up in the back of the van developed the band's team spirit and sense of discipline. And in the spirit of alleviating the boredom, their sense of humour developed too.

ZAL: We could be quite daft. We'd turn up for our residency at the Electric Gardens, do half a show as Tear Gas, go off, shave off our heavy metal beards, and dress up as Johnny Rocket and the Zoomers then go back on as this different band...

TED: Roadies John and Rab played these two characters, Sid and Bovey. John used to wear a mask on the top of his head so he was looking down but the mask was facing forward – it was quite freaky. If Chris and I were sitting in a transport cafe, and there were people we didn't know sitting nearby, Rab would come up to us as if he was a stranger and he'd say, 'I'm skint, are you finished with those beans?' We'd say, 'Aye, help yourself,' and he'd rub them into his hair...

We used to make up these games to relieve the boredom on long journeys. There was one where you had to substitute a word in a movie title with the word 'frog'. You had 'Ben Frog' or 'Frog Hur' but every now and again someone would come up with the one-word title 'Frog'... They knew where they were in their head... The worry was if you got it too. But there was always something to talk about, and always loads of scud books lying around the back of the van...

It was this final Tear Gas lineup that headed to London in early 1972 to play a gig with Alex Harvey. The Marquee show came about because Eddie was working for Bill Fehilly's company, Mountain Managements. Mountain looked after Nazareth and Alex at the time, and were thinking about spreading wings. It may well be that the notion of a tie-up had already been discussed.

ZAL: No one had primed us about this, though. As far as we were concerned it was a gig in the Marquee and it didn't matter who was headlining. Eddie will have had something to do with it – typical underhand political subversive capitalist shit. Chess with real people. I felt like a bishop a lot of the time – well, I didn't want to be a knight, did I? Or a pawn...

TED: You might have made a good queen after the tights experiences.

ZAL: I know about tights. Extra-thick gusset, I'll have you know.

TED: Well, it had to take a sock, didn't it?

ZAL: A hiking sock...

It was an interesting evening. The club wasn't particularly busy, and consisted equally of Alex fans and Tear Gas fans. During set-up and soundcheck Ted became aware that Alex was wandering round about them, asking what keys they played in, what they thought of their gear and so on. Looking back, he's sure they were being sussed out.

Tear Gas played their set and then it was the turn of Alex's three-piece outfit, whose primitive progressive sound turned out to be very unconvincing, although ideas like Isobel Goudie and Hammer Song were in there. In the natural way of things, each act had an opinion of each other; but maybe Alex's was more important at the time.

He would later say: 'I think they can play and I know they can sing and write songs. The problem was, when I met Tear Gas they were playing a thousand different things at the same time. I try to be simple and strip things down to the basics. There are so many ideas you can't use them all – you have to skim the cream.'

EDDIE: He was doing all that hippy stuff, the Giant Moth era and afterwards... but he was loved. You have no idea how much Alex was loved in London, even then – everyone who was anyone knew Alex Harvey.

TED: At the soundcheck Alex came up on stage and he walked among us. Yes! The Faith Healer walked among us!

ZAL: I don't remember that – I'd have ignored him anyway. I was very shy.

TED: I was disappointed how watery his band sounded compared to us – but I was impressed with Alex. I remember thinking, there's something about him, something dangerous and attractive... I didn't go looking for this kind of stuff so I was surprised to find myself thinking it. Charisma's the easiest way to describe it, but it's not quite there. Still, his band weren't doing anything for him - it wasn't a musical experience for the boys. But he just captured me. I remember a mate of mine was in the dressing room asking me in a loud voice, 'So who the fuck's this old bastard Alex Harvey meant ti' be?' and Alex was standing behind him. I should have introduced them, really...

CHRIS: I don't remember much of his set – I was probably away posing somewhere. And you have to remember I was deaf for two hours after our set! But it seemed very... polite, and it was all bluesy. Later on Alex told me, if an audience aren't listening to you go up close to the mic and start muttering, and people will shut up to try and hear what you're saying. That's how to get attention... Mind you, it seemed a bit strange that he knew how to get attention, but once he'd got it his band weren't worth it. I think he maybe realised he could take our in-yer-face thing and make anything out of it. I think he saw a bigger picture than any of us, and he'd have seen himself in front of it, and thought, if I can put a brake on this runaway train we can go places. We were just blasting out of control down the track while Alex saw all the branch lines – if you can play this then you'll be able to play that, and so on.

That show, however, was just another one in thousands, and Tear Gas thought no more about it at the time. They had something else on their minds anyway: their future. Hugh had brought that vital missing element into the music. Dave had written some lyrics and Hugh and Zal had begun working on music. There was a new creative energy. But it was going to be strangled at birth, because the band were about to split up.

• PLUS NME FREE GIG THIS WEEK:

ALEX HARVEY TEAR GAS

THE THIRD in the new series of NME/Marquee Free nights takes place next Wednesday and features the new ALEX HARVEY BAND, TEAR GAS and German group EULENSPYGEL.

As before, these NME Wednesday nights are free to readers and their friends, but get along early because the club, in Wardour Street, W.1, has a limited capacity and is invariably packed to the rafters.

Remember to take along the adjacent coupon which allows priority admission to NME readers.

A word on the bands:

ALEX HARVEY, after 15 years in the business, is now back on the road. Until six weeks ago, he was a force in the "Hair" band, having joined at the musical's inception, but now has left to form his own group again.

Concentrating as usual on tough, original music, Harvey will be on guitar and vocals, his two backing musicians being Ian Ellis, bass, and Dave Dufort, drums.

TEAR GAS are a 5-strong Scottish group, very much in the hard-rock category. They've been around for a couple of years now, and have one album to their credit.

West German group EULENSPYGEL is making its first visit to Britain, basically to record a second album here. Their first, oddly, was titled "Eulenspygel 2." Very much in the Chicago bag, the seven-piece outfit consists of two guitars (one of whom doubles on violin), flute, organ, bass, harmonica and drums.

ALEX HARVEY

NME sponsored the event at which Alex and Tear Gas met

TED: Hugh in the band made things a lot better. The elements were all there – the four-stroke engine was running at the right kind of, em, engine-type thing...

ZAL: Oh aye, nepotism rears its ugly head! Actually, what's sad about that is we never got the chance to record with that lineup, take the four-stroke out for a spin and see what it could do.

HUGH: I introduced a lot of Tamla Motown – Hugo decides Motown's coming back! The management of the Electric Gardens wanted people to be dancing all night, and I thought Motown would keep them on their feet. We spent about a month learning about 20 of them. In the end it didn't make people dance any more or less, but there you go.

CHRIS: I remember we did Cleethorpes, supporting the Pink Fairies, then when we went back we headlined and a band called Jude supported us – Frankie Miller, Robin Trower, Jimmy Dewar and

Clive Bunker – supporting us! So that's an example of how successful we were. In a club of four or five hundred people it was fine, we could get away with it. But in bigger venues it became obvious we had limitations. We didn't have a PA system for a start.

ZAL: We'd done the teenybop stuff in the Bo Weavles – we didn't want to be popular and do singles. We wanted to record albums and never come out of the cellar for months. But we were doing the same gigs! Some of the fans migrated with us, the ones who could stomach it... But as we started getting darker, getting into that groove, we had fewer girls and more guys coming to see us. Everyone would sit down, get stoned and watch. No one was dancing. A real different scenario. People were waiting for the dancing to start, no one was smiling at anyone, and the venue wouldn't have us back. It became limiting: the gigs became more elitist. You were thrashing out your own little thing, you had your blinkers on and your head down because you wanted to be in your own world... You get your bit right, I'll get mine, and it'll be okay. Listen to Hendrix – it's disparate, people are going for it all over the place.

And some of our material didn't come up to scratch, never mind the other pressures. It wasn't strong enough to be big league. At the time we were giving it pelters, doing the right thing. But there was a lack of originality in a lot of what we did. We couldn't see the light of day, while more and more people were saying to us, we don't want you back here because people can't dance to you.

They were still making up to £400 per show, but once the gear payments were made there wasn't much left. Out of the remains, a lot of it went on funding shows in England, where the band slept in transport cafes and did anything else they could to keep expenses down. They paid themselves just £8 a week (Zal took a little more because he was married) and found themselves in stalemate.

At a make-or-break meeting, Eddie told them they'd come to the end of the road. If they played 20 more gigs they'd have the gear paid off, but there was nothing else positive to be said for playing 20 more gigs in the fewer and fewer places that wanted them. The musical potential wasn't going to be realised. Tear Gas was over.

EDDIE: By 1971 the band were on a plateau. They were incredible, they'd played everywhere, but they just weren't making it. Everyone was just waiting for something to happen. Bill Fehilly had already taken Derek Nichol to London with Nazareth, and he was pouring money into them. Then Bill asked me, can you find a band for Alex? The band he had was terrible. He knew it, he was pished, he was offending people, but there was something about him even in that condition. So I thought, Tear Gas and Alex Harvey? Nooooo... And Bill said, I've got millions – I'll support the band. So I thought, Tear Gas and Alex Harvey? Sounds like a great band!

TED: Eddie told us, we have one possible avenue of salvation. Remember that guy Alex Harvey? you'll be taken on by Mountain. You'll be on a retainer – a retainer! – of £15 a week. And your gear will be paid off. And Alex has a lot of experience, he knows everyone... I remember standing on the platform at Anniesland station, waiting for the train home, and saying to Hugh: 'Well, at least it'll keep the band together.' Because we're assuming we'll have to play stuff we don't want to play. It was the only positive thing I could hold onto, because I remembered what his band was like at the Marquee. I was confident we could handle it somehow. Somehow...

Z THE ENDS OF THE PERM

ZAL ON THE TEAR GAS ALBUMS

Piggy-Go-Getter perfectly highlights the transition the Bo-Weavles made from soul and funk to a more progressive musical style. You can still hear the remnants of those early influences on certain tracks but the overall intent is to play things with a definite rock feel. What we appear to have stumbled upon is a bizarre form of American west-coast prog-rock. There's nothing ragged here, but its immediate shortcoming is in trying to appeal to everyone and their Granny.

Lost Awakening: Angst-ridden vaporous ramble with some over zealous whammy-bar.
Your Woman's Gone and Left You: Pleasant feel and slinky bass playing; however the guitar licks belong in the drawer marked 'Knitwear'.
Night Girl: A budding musical perhaps, though again I'd raise the question of such abundant harmonies. Fine rock–blues guitar and Hammond.
Nothing Can Change Your Mind: Pure fromage, the sun-tanned clone of Andy Williams and the Association.
Living For Today: A fine wholesome riff — this track would actually stand up for victims of today's retro fetish.
Big House: A fair attempt at some down-home country rock.
Mirrors of Sorrow: Another crack at the heavy-funk elements of archetypal 60's prog rock (Jeff Beck, Deep Purple and so on). Superb openly-animated drum track.
Look What Else is Happening: A keen, raucous start with some acute protest lyrics, and then it's up, up and away with the Fifth Dimension before Zal's jazzy, Wes Montgomery interlude that rudely ends up ripping the arse out of something akin to Deep Purple.
I'm Fallin' Far Behind: More heavy funk and steamy guitar passed through a cocktail cabinet. Actually it's a Leslie.
Witches Come Today: This is another stand-out track, with lashings of the right atmosphere and some no-nonsense aggression. Interestingly, as a last track it seems also to point the way forward.

As a second album Tear Gas admirably qualifies the progressive intentions of Piggy. In fact, I think it robustly sets out to compensate for the first album's misgivings. It's a vibrant mix of genuine inventiveness, again hampered only by a lack of finesse in its production and, occasionally, execution. By this time Eddie Campbell had left (or was he pushed), though to this day I can't recall why. Ted had joined us and throughout the album you can hear what a clear contribution he makes to many of the fearsome arrangements. I've also heard people say that the guitar playing is as good as it gets for the time. I won't comment on that except to say it was a proving ground, if you like, for my own development. So, wave goodbye to those sycophantic harmonies, and wolf down some serious guitar biscuits...

That's What's Real: Guitar wise it's a saucy array of riffs propped up with a spunky, if slightly nomadic, little solo. Some clear attention to detail within the overall arrangement though, including the vocals.

Love Story: A pleasing if effusive tribute to Tull, who we all admired as a band of real musical ability.

Lay It On Me: An eager, catchy shuffle. Some rare bottleneck guitar from the would-be boy wonder while Chris and Ted lay down the foundations of a now legendary rhythm section.

Woman For Sale: A commendable throbalong riff that's still great to play. And a stand-out chorus from Dave. Tense, mutilated guitar work that's not always in perfect pitch. The ending is the kind of flash, bare-breasted action we were prone to exhibit at gigs.

I'm Glad: In which smart lyric wrestles with yet another iron-fisted riff. Executive guitar solo section involving some kind of oblique harmonic calamity. The middle-eight proves what a great singer Dave is when he can hear himself. But is this really a boy meets or boy meats girl story?

Where Is My Answer: Dave's tour de force. Perhaps my favourite Tear Gas song, it's arguably the most accomplished track on the album — progressive rock with all its adornment.

Jailhouse Rock/All Shook Up: A rabid live recording, and it's a Beck rip-off almost note for note, strapped to a rhythm section gloriously perched on the edge of derision.

The First Time: An apposite musical opus that yet again persuades us of the metaphysical nature of the human race, a reality woven from the emblematic poetry that proves the extent to which man's overwhelming thirst for sex runs parallel to being a rock musician. Garlanded with a stunning finale from Ronnie Leahy on Hammond.

PART TWO

VAMBO ROOL

We've never had
a hit... but we
insist on the
red carpet at
the airport

SAHB's first official photo, June 1972: Ted, Hugh, Zal, Alex and Chris

1 FRAMED

'HOWFF' is an old Scots word for a drinking den, and the Burns Howff in Glasgow's West Regent Street was an old Scots place for musicians to play and hang out. That's where Tear Gas waited until Alex arrived, dressed like a coollege professor in a corduroy jacket with elbow patches, with his guitar strapped over his back. There was a short conversation – he may or may not have bought them a drink – and they proceeded to Thor Studios to put their music where their mouths were.

TED: Alex said: 'Okay, I've got this song called Midnight Moses – be careful with it, because it's not quite as straightforward as you think.' So everyone picked up their bits and we went through it, and I thought, yeah, we can play this.

ZAL: He'd been doing what he did, and I hadn't been impressed – this is out of tune, he's not singing that very well... but when we got a hold of Midnight Moses it all changed. He was just bouncing about with his manic grin and there was a real buzz about it: about him as a performer. He had so much conviction about what he had in the bag – he had the material, he had the presentation – he just needed the backing.

HUGH: My impression is that Alex knew what he wanted from the word 'go'. I recall playing Midnight Moses that day, the solid eight-part on the right hand, and thinking it was kinda boring, there was no opportunity for me to show off... But it turned out it was harder to keep going than I'd thought.

They also ran through Framed and I Just Wanna Make Love To You that day, but it was the instant bite of Midnight Moses that grabbed them. Alex would later say: 'When I met them they were playing a thousand different things at the same time, while I try to be simple, so we stripped it down a bit. I don't think the band could believe they played like that.'

DAVE: They were trying I Just Wanna Make Love To You and Zal was doing the guitar part, and Alex was saying, no, turn it down, turn it down. Of course, anything lower than 11 and it wasn't happening for us. You could hear the guitar from the body as loud as the amp – but Zal stayed with it, and once the tiptoe dynamic was established, there was everywhere to go. That was a big big lesson to us all.

But there were still doubts – and in some views there'd always be doubts – about what was going on. The main thing was that nothing else was going on, for Tear Gas or Alex, and so with a jumpstart like this both parties decided to give it a bash.

CHRIS: It was just relief – it could have been the last, never mind first, rehearsal – but we realised we could still do the Fear Gas thing. We worried we'd be made to tone it down later on – we didn't

		JUNE 1972	a.m.	JUNE 1972		p.m.	
THU	1	Code *lofu flav.*		*Burns Howff*		1	*lo*
FRI	2			*Liverpool*		2	
SAT	3					3	
SUN	4			*Cumnock*		4	
MON	5	*Meet Mr Ichiley.*				5	
TUE	6					6	
WED	7			*Burns Howff*		7	
THU	8					8	
FRI	9	*Meet Alex Harvey*		*Rehearsal 2-8.*		9	
SAT	10	*Burns Howff*		*Germinal One*		10	
SUN	11	*Rehearsal 2-6*				11	
MON	12					12	
TUE	13					13	
WED	14	*J.M. Ballroom*		*Dance*		14	
THU	15					15	
FRI	16					16	
						17	

Ted's diary records Tear Gas' meeting with Bill and the first rehearsal with Alex

realise that's exactly what Alex liked about us. So afterwards we went to the pub and asked each other, was that alright for you? And it was. Alex could easily have said, I want you to play that and you to play that, and it would have been, hello I must be leaving...

It was about this time, very early in the new band's development, that Les Harvey died on stage. He was on tour with Stone The Crows, the band he'd started with Maggie Bell. Preparing for a show at Swansea Top Rank Ballroom, Les made contact with a live mic while touching his guitar, received a huge electric shock and was killed instantly.

Alex never got over the tragedy. He'd always been close to his brother – so much so they had an almost psychic connection. They used to turn up at the same place without having made arrangements to meet. Alex had taught Les to play the guitar, bringing the shy young boy out of his shell and giving him the skill to use his huge musical talent.

Somehow Alex kept it together as he dealt with most of the funeral arrangements. Friends suggest he was trying to stay strong for his mum, while others believe Bill provided the support he needed, and there's no doubt his loving family were there for him. But whether it was a method of therapy, or to build a fitting tribute for his lost brother, Alex threw himself into his work and set a pace that saw SAHB thrown into a manic fury of gigging, writing and recording which would last five years.

CHRIS: Alex didn't talk about it much to us. It wasn't a taboo subject – it was mentioned but it was best left alone. It was a great thing for Alex when Tam Fairgrieve came on board backstage, because he was a master electrician. Tam ran about with his wee meter all the time, checking it was impossible to get even a wee static discharge. Alex was really grateful for that. If anyone said they'd had a wee shock, like putting the key in the hotel room door, it always got a reaction from Alex. He was conscious of it all the time. There were points every now and again when something would ding off the Leslie thing, some tenuous link or other would send him off into a morose mood.
TED: It didn't come up till we went to Swansea. We'd gone down a storm – it was one of the first

nights it all really came together. Everyone was in the bar except Alex, so I went into the dressing room to join him, and he started to cry. I got really emotional too, because he hadn't shown any emotion until then.

ZAL: Philosophical's not the word, but he had an outlook, a broad view, and everything fitted in; so something like this was part of it. When you knew him offstage, he was very deep, very intellectual, very concerned about everything... A lot of it's in the songs – wonderful messages. Death was something he was prepared to go along with, but he never got over these things.

SLOWLY but surely, the band began working on developing a set. The vast majority came from Alex's bag of tricks, soul and blues songs he'd written or covered in the past; but all the time everyone was working on a dynamic shape for the band. In between times, Tear Gas continued to play and Alex fulfilled his Hair commitments, with pre-Tubular Mike Oldfield depping for him when he came north to join in the fun with his new bandmates. Although the definition of 'fun' was arguable. Maybe it was the age gap – Alex was nearly 17 years older than the others; or maybe it was the way Tear Gas fans booed Alex...

TED: When we played at Clouds we didn't have enough material to do a whole set with Alex. So he was going to do an acoustic thing, and that's when people started shouting at him. And he started shouting back, calling them everything under the sun. My heart sank – I thought, that's it, that's the band split, it's not going to happen – but Alex loved it.

CHRIS: So the audience are fucked off, we're fucked off, Bill's fucked off – because he thought we were too loud and it still said 'Tear Gas' on the bass drum – and Alex is going about celebrating... A bad reaction's better than no reaction. During the Soul Band era, his hire purchase company wrote to him and said, start making payments again or we'll put your name in the paper. Alex wrote back saying, dear sirs, we're skint but we'd love the publicity if you'd be so kind as to put us in the paper... All publicity was good.

Never mind the band – Tear Gas fans remained to be convinced. There was an early gig at St Andrews, supporting Arthur Brown and what he called his new 'commercial' set, consisting of his band painting themselves gold and Arthur himself being rolled on stage in a huge syringe – which, Spinal Tap style, he got stuck in. Alex arrived in a stookie, claiming he'd broken his leg, and performed in a wheelchair; but the jury's still out over the escapade. After the show, a couple of guys in the bar asked to speak to Ted and Chris; they understood this wee guy Harvey had heavy-mobbed his way into Tear Gas, and if the band required heavy-mob help to remove him again, there were several dozen volunteers waiting.

At another early show Chris was attacked after a disagreement over a girl. On hearing the news, Alex marched on stage during the support band's set and demanded to know who was responsible, taking his belt off and threatening to destroy the whole audience unless the culprit was surrendered. It was a taste of things to come.

Work progressed, and the guys began to get a handle on Alex's musical philosophy. Their hard rock influences meant they were fans of outfits like Vanilla Fudge, Little Feat, Frank Zappa and so forth; but he asked them: 'Why do you want to to that? *They're* doing that – we should be doing something different.' Alex wanted to include the benefits of the band's wide-ranging influences, but he wanted to use them to break new ground. This self-motivational attitude was soon to be expressed in the band's name.

Framed promo pic: Chris, Zal, Hugh and Ted with Harvey the singer in front and Harvey the jakey on the right

TED: The way Alex put it was, we've got to let people know what they're going to get. If we say it's going to be something, we're gonny have to be it. So we'll call it the Sensational Alex Harvey Band, and what I mean by that is: we've got to be sensational.

CHRIS: This lineup was such a change for Alex as well. There had been other Alex Harvey Bands but there needed to be something else. I remember saying, we're setting ourselves up here – writers will say, Sensational? We'll be the judge of that... It was very brave, I thought. I remember the discussion, going through the fabulous this, the wonderful that, and he said, The Sensational Alex Harvey Band – that's it! I wasn't sure, but then at the time we still thought it might be a one-album wonder. You wouldn't really call it sensational, not until well after Framed; but now we started having to think about things that made us sensational...

EDDIE: When you heard him announcing it, it worked – it's a great title to announce.

IN the early 70s record labels had a more lenient approach to a band's first album: the point of it was to have a product to tour with, and use the experience to gel the band's abilities; and the money would start coming in with the second album. Nowadays, of course, bands are dropped when their first album doesn't make enough profit. So when plans were put in place to start touring seriously in December of 1972, it seemed perfectly natural to cut a disc of the old Alex standards the band had been playing up until then.

Framed was recorded in three days at Morgan Studios in London. During these lightning-speed sessions SAHB developed an approach to recording that served them well in years to come. The mainstay was knowing the material inside out, playing it together as fresh and as lively as possible, and adding the bare minimum of overdubs to the raw noise. Fast and honest. The laid-back vibe on a track like I Just Wanna Make Love To You was achieved because the band knew exactly what they were about: they weren't recording, they were *performing*. The result is a great album – even if the technical side of recording lets it down a tad.

CHRIS: The quality of recording really dates it – but the playing is good.

TED: The sound of my kit had been emasculated on Tear Gas, and that had been annoying because I was proud of my drum sound and people used to compliment me on it all the time.

CHRIS: And then these people got taken away in ambulances.

TED: I made sure I got a lot closer to my sound this time. But the vocal sound they got for Alex was wrong. It was too boxy and dry. I was always very aware of Alex's lyrics – they inspired me as I played. Some of these great lyrics don't come out clearly enough.

CHRIS: Yeah, it did end up like, Alex Harvey's voice also appears on this album. They saw it as part of the music instead of the main feature, and we'd arranged the songs round his voice. I'd love to get hold of the original tapes and mix it properly... We were all chuffed with it, though.

ZAL: Big Louis is a song I never understood at the time. I was thinking, should we be playing this? We did a lot of that, wondering if it was really stuff we should be doing. But when we played it in the 90s it suddenly occurred to me how interesting the song was.

TED: I remember in the car park at Morgan Studios, Alex and Chris suggested to me quite strongly that I take a drink. Southern Comfort and coke, they said, is just like a milkshake and you won't even know you're turning into an alcoholic... Up till then I didn't drink, but they saw to that...

The band visited the double-shite end of the Gorbals for the cover shots, scrabbling about in the semi-demolished tenement rubble for props. The uncredited sixth member on the sleeve was a jakey called, appropriately enough, Harvey, who wandered over, decided he was enjoying the proceedings and stayed for the duration. Alex borrowed his glasses for the shoot and Ted bought his belt buckle, and wore it for many years afterwards. As a touching epitaph, Harvey's mum saw the album sleeve and was re-united with a son she thought had been long dead.

Melody Maker were kind but neutral about Framed, suggesting perhaps that the reviewer may not have seen the band live. 'Framed,' they noted, 'gets the album off in fine style but lacks the magical touch possessed by the Coasters' original version'.

It was early days, though, and very soon afterwards no one had an excuse not to have seen SAHB. In November they made their first TV appearances including their premiere on the Old Grey Whistle Test, launching a series of legendary appearances with Whispering Bob Harris. In between these TV shows they commenced their first full-scale UK tour, and it wasn't long before the reviewers began to notice the difference between a pinkish-sleeved vinyl disc and five fuck-off Glaswegians giving it laldy in your face. The NME cottoned on early: 'The Fantastic [sic] Alex Harvey Band gave entertainment rather than a technical display of musical prowess – and that, after all, is what live rock should be all about. Evil is the best word to describe the demonic stage presence of Harvey himself.' And instead of slating the recorded version of Framed, Roger St Pierre praised the way Alex 'came closer than anyone I've seen before to the brash womanising evoked by the Chicago blues greats'.

Every live appearance was a learning experience. SAHB were picking up every lesson fast, and turning their collective knowledge into a powerhouse of presentational mastery. And they were gradually getting used to each other's little foibles.

ZAL: Before every show Alex would do his exercises, do his headstand then go and start screaming at himself in the mirror: Cunts! *Cunts!* **Cunts!** He got himself really wound up. It was scary until you got used to it.

EDDIE: When we saw Joe Walsh at the Electric Gardens, that was the first time we heard a JBL sound system. Our first impression of a real sound. You could feel it in your chest at the back of the hall, and we were like, fuck's sake, gie's wan o'them... We got one and it broke down on the first night. Bill was a little upset: What the fuck have I spent my money on?

TED: But there was one night the sound came together and we all really felt it. So on the way home we all stripped naked in the van and ran into a field in the morning sunlight, and we thought this was hilarious... We got back into the van, still naked, and drove into a wee village for petrol. Chris and I got out and grabbed a bike we'd seen then pedalled round the village, totally bollock! It was the sheer euphoria of the gig. We thought everything was hilarious... The idea of being rock stars was hilarious.

Nevertheless, it was shortly about to be.

Z MURKY MELANGE OF FLAWLESS RAPPORT

ZAL ON FRAMED

Those relentless soulful days, followed by the grim, iron–fisted riffs... fuckin' great!If he had uttered those words a day or two before, Z would have offered himself a simple, restrained smile. And then SAHB came along and immediately he caught sight of himself falling into the weird workings of some monstrous machine...

One thing though was for sure. It was the kind of moment that filled you with intense delight. A murky mélange of flawless rapport and salubrious union that just oozed fun. It was a concoction as fantastic as the senses.

Though he understood the real world perfectly well, its virtues and its abundant clues, Alex always gave the impression he wasn't interested in being safe and sorry; and he wouldn't let self–pity mess up his innate, recaptured sense of denial. Easier, he thought, to abide by the sexier path of deprivation.

And that's exactly how *Framed* opens with its title track: a senile blues adaptation of the Leiber and Stoller classic of the late 50s, Alex revelling in the theatrics of the pre–nuclear story line. Adulatory solo, complete with the old frozen–finger finish; a snail–paced riff and a bruising, nightclub ending.

Hammer Song announces itself with what is still a fine mood swing. Our new version is purely for those of a nervous disposition.

Midnight Moses roars into life like a rampant bluenose, the iron–fisted riff again rearing its rosy head. 'Can you play this riff?' he said. 'What, *this* riff?' Z battered it out. Almost immediately Alex was bouncing in an elegant pair of black brothel creepers, guitar tucked up in the stramash, swaying from side to side like the seventh son. Which reminds me of the time I watched his lordship, clambering through the pines, guitar slung over his back, aimed at serenading a likely–looking daughter and her daughter. He looked keen enough for a three-day cross-country skiing event.

Isobel Goudie is the song of everyone's youth. Hunting lads on the prowl for something approach–ing a cross between your pork–bellied granny and the loins of eternal youth. Authenticity as to its origins unfold through the track's overall edginess and production arrangement. If Tear Gas fans hated Alex, this would do him exactly fuck–all good in trying to conquer their apoplexy.

Buff's Bar Blues is what inspired us all in the first place, especially Alex. Tear Gas again set up the ideal backdrop to a joyfully sub–academic lyric from Alex. Z was thinking, maybe this old cunt can still sing...

I Just Wanna Make Love To You... Try to imagine things were changing by this point. Business, until now uneasy, suddenly becomes a thing of delight. Playing on tracks like this, with Alex's mates in the horn section, was a fine lesson indeed. Our confidence was overflowing and the doom and gloom became a pale, haphazard memory...

Mountain gave us a big break. There were posters and pleasure domes, pages of fame – and pressed silver and gold plated platters. They gave you that initial feeling of success – anyone who saw them immediately assumed you were rich and famous. The discs cost about five krim each. What they spelled out though, what was written on them, gives the game away: in terms of record sales their value was in excess of a million krim.

The Big Mountain...

So there you have it, in the final chase, as the song says. Some shit, eh? And I suppose songs like *Hole In Her Stocking* and *Big Louie* didn't always convince you the path would be paved with sweat–encrusted maidens wallowing at your feet. But then, the likes of *St Anthony* made up for those less inspired moments and kept us on our toes, interested.

Anyway, the janitor was paid. The tarts were despatched, in sequence, at a place of their choosing; they actually thanked us. And we drove all the way in this lashing rain, into a tyrant's night, when everything starts to get funny and blurred at the edges and suddenly it becomes silent and still.

It was Nightmare City! A headline gig. Things were happening fast. And thoughts of rationing out a fiver a week were quickly replaced with discussions about musical direction and what colour of hair to choose, like articulate animals trying to encounter something bewildering. It set the pulses racing to glimpse at what until now had only been part of the imagination. We enteredthe city terrified of nothing, as gangs must sometimes feel.. It was time to get dressed up. Smothered in bravado and a blend of morose poses and disarming grimaces, Z took to it like a duck to buns.

We found a hotel near Rent–a–rectum Square, Peregrine and Meredith banging on the walls every night. It was suitably close to the Mountain. Alex looked hell–bent on survival and livened things up with the occasional bare–knuckle barbecue down the Speakeasy.

Every day we joined the other insects, lined up by the entrance as part of a team working to excavate the Rock Drill, taking turns to pass the scalding earth back through a small opening that was now only a few steps from the core itself. The work made us a strong unit and no matter where we found ourselves, we still remained the boys from SAHB...

2 NEXT

SEVERAL thousand people knew the secret by now, and by the end of 1973 several tens of thousands of people were going to be sharing it. The year began with just a little time to reflect, and then a major act of commitment on everyone's part: the guys moved down to London.

In the first instance they lived in Nazareth's flat while their stablemates were in the USA, and in early months flittered between that and the Durand Hotel. Even so, they were only a few miles from Alex's house, and so SAHB had the opportunity to begin doing things as a band, and really get to work on developing some sensational character.

TED: The day we were leaving Alex came to visit my parents. My dad was a tough man, a steelworker, a very sharp guy; and he said to Alex, are you gonny look after my boy? It was only afterwards I understood the significance, but Alex would have seen it at the time. I'd been to London with the Dream Police but this was the real deal – I wasn't coming back for 21 years. It made me think of that old song, The Gallowa'Hills, the bit about leaving your old land for a new country, for better or worse.

CHRIS: Up until then it had still been Tear Gas and Alex, but this is when it became SAHB. And when the deal was done, we were being paid £50 a week – palm trees were waving! To put that in context, a Jaguar XJ12 cost £3500 at the time – now it's about £55,000...

They were young boys on the make, and they had it large when time permitted. They became a regular fixture at the Speakeasy, mixing with Jeff Beck, the Jam, Motorhead, John Entwistle, Peter Green, Giner Baker – in those days there was no pecking order and no teams of minders. The most you had was one roadie, and he was there to stop you making an arse of yourself rather than to stop people approaching you.

Soon they moved into their own flat, customised to get the right number of bedrooms, and the domestic bliss didn't begin at all.

TED: They just got it customised so they could stay up till four in the morning, partying, doing drugs and listening to music while I was trying to sleep. That's why I started taking drugs...

CHRIS: See, this is the kind of shite that comes out. Anyway, I was in the room above the lounge so I had to put up with the noise too...

TED: No you didn't – you were in the lounge making the noise!

CHRIS: Aye, well... that's true.

But we were all in this flat. My wife moved down, Davie's wife moved down – Zal's wife didn't because they already had a house in Glasgow and she was working. But we had all these Scottish lads and lassies, then Ted's American girlfriend moved in. And no offence to anyone, but there's a culture–shock going on there. She was intense, she was a vegan, what star sign are you, don't tell me, you're a capricorn, no... And after ten guesses: I knew it! Zal and I used to say we were asparagus with broccoli rising. And you couldn't be cancer, because of the illness – you had to be a moonchild...

TED: But going over for dinner with Trudy and Alex was great fun. They were a lot of fun as a couple. The first time we went round Zal pretended to be an Australian who'd been in a car crash and had mental problems as a result. Alex loved it! We had all these sketches that had grown through the years. Another one was Zal playing the part of this cool guy leaning against a bar, and he'd act out chatting up a bird, then ask her to leave with him, and when he moved away from the bar he'd walk in the leaning shape, as if he was stuck in it... Bill thought it was hilarious, and he'd get Zal to do it everywhere we went.

Despite the band's burgeoning social life, work continued on defining its attitude and character. Alex encouraged belief in the material and reliance on the team ethic. The band ran with it, and the harlequin Zal and punk Chris were born.

TED: When we did Framed we aimed to play it heavy and slow it down – and in the end I couldn't believe how slow we did it. I got off on starting the beat because the audience were going mad. It was like time stopped. And then when the music came in it was astonishing – toes were curling, we were saying, we're gonny fuckin' play it this slow, *right*? If you all believe it, it works. Magic happens. And Alex noised me up about the things that used to bug me: There's a screw loose on the hihat? Well, fuck, the concert's cancelled... I got his point. If I wasn't playing hard enough he'd turn round and growl at me, and hit cymbals till I got back into it. Feel something – he taught me that right away. It doesn't matter what you feel as long as you feel something and pour it into your playing. The audience won't feel anything if you don't.

CHRIS: We used to do lots of things as a band – we went to see Cabaret, we went to Paris to see Alcazar and we began to see what the professionals could do with a show. Of course we had to find a way of doing it while keeping the costs down.

ZAL: It was part of the tounge-in-cheek thing, all the choreography. It was nothing new – the Shadows used to dance, but it appealed to us because you had this heavy band people were intimidated by, then when you went on stage you'd have them rolling in the aisles with the mad dance routine. Bill could see the potential of the presentation. We were playing the Marquee and he told me, from the back of the hall I can't see the faces you're making. Why don't you try doing something to your face? I started out with green dots stuck all over my face, but eventually someone suggested painting it white, and as soon as it was said I knew, yeah, that works.

TED: Alex wanted to bring out the characters, like a comic book, so people could easily identify the statements that were being made. We started getting these ideas together.

CHRIS: He nailed it down by saying, it's not going to work of you make people wear clothes that take away from their personality. I didn't ever like the top of my outfit, but the codpiece was brilliant – I'd always had problems hitting the Fender precision off my bollocks, and the way I used to stand with my legs apart it really hurt. Bambi, our designer, said, why don't you wear a codpiece outside your trousers? I said, what, like Alas Poor Yorick? She said she could make it look good. The first few times I wore it I was a bit self-conscious but it was a great idea.

ZAL: The thing we all liked about the costumes was the material was all matte – there was nothing shiny and glittery. They looked like Vaudeville or circus outfits. A lot of bands had started dressing

What nearly to wear: above, Ted, Zal, Alex, Chris and Hugh as the
outfits and makeup take shape; and below, Alex as a lounge lizard

The Sensational
ALEX HARVEY BAND

at the MARQUEE
WEDNESDAY JUNE 20th
featuring
BIG BAD BUD'S
BRASS
ADMIT TWO

up, so we were trying to avoid being lumped in with the glam rock thing. Alex liked the way we achieved that. He found his own things to wear as well, but he managed to keep the torn jeans, the pump-up shoes and the t-shirt thing. It made us different.

Once and for all the gap between Alex and Tear Gas had been bridged. There was a gang on stage, and while there had always been plenty to watch with the frontman doing his thing, there was even more to it now. The interplay between Alex and Zal became a mainstay of the show, with each fighting the other for the limelight. Both characters fed off it and became the larger for it. And for sheer domination factor, it was hard to beat Chris, Alex and Zal with their left feet on the monitors, leering into the crowd as they thundered through Midnight Moses. They looked huge, they looked hard, and you didn't dare take your eyes off them. All these elements came together in the set-pieces between songs; and musical set-pieces came into the show early too. There was a big slow dramatic opening to St Anthony, after which Alex would open his book to tell the audience a story; and meanwhile Chris and Zal came up from behind and took their places on either side of him, staring the crowd out, daring them to stop paying attention. In another opener the frontline boys would hit a chord then march one step forward, hit another and step forward again, and keep going until they were at the front of the stage – by which time the audience had taken the same number of steps back.

TED: We did one gig and at the end there was nothing but almost total silence – we'd known something was going on because the audience hadn't taken their eyes off us the whole show. It was a long walk to the dressing room but soon after we arrived, Dick, our tour manager, said, you'd better get back on – they're going wild. It wasn't until we'd left the stage folk turned round to their mates and said, what you think of that – wasn't it brilliant? We didn't even have Faith Healer at the time, but it was really beginning to work.

This was the show that hit the road in February 1973, and found itself supporting Mott the Hoople for five dates. Ian Hunter's outfit were at the top of their game and SAHB fitted in perfectly to the show. It was a huge step up in terms of audience size, and the guys made the most of their opportunity.

Zal remembers Mick Ralphs inviting him up to join in Mott's encore at the Birmingham Town Hall. Chris remembers wondering why the city of Birmingham didn't have a city hall. Ian Dickson, a photographer who was to work with SAHB in an official capacity several times in the future, remembers offering a very grateful Alex some pictures of his dead brother: 'I turned up at the gig with a boxful of prints of Les and said, I'd like you to have them. He was very touched.'

By now SAHB were hungry for a real challenge, and it came in the form of supporting Slade on a UK tour. If Mott had been at the top of their game, Slade were at the top of everyone else's. It's difficult to describe how big Noddy and co were in mid-73. They'd been at the forefront of the glam look, they put a lot of fun into their show – and, more importantly, they could play like fuck. No one else dared to take the support slot.

SAHB, naturally, jumped at the chance.

ZAL: The audience were young and they loved rock, and they were there to see Slade from the beginning of the night. It wasn't the type of audience who went for a drink while the support act were on – they were up for it the moment the doors opened. So when we started playing there was a buzz – love you or hate you, it didn't matter...

CHRIS: We knew them from Ambrose Slade when they'd been skinheads. Great guys, and a great band. But our music wasn't exactly compatible... their fans were covered in glitter and top hats with Skweez Me Pleez Me written on them, and they just didn't want us. So Alex said, let's antagonise them. And they loved it! They were throwing things and Alex was squirting them with water pistols. When we played Blackburn he filled the pistols with his own piss, and the front rows were standing with their mouths open when he squirted them... But it was all more like pantomime – there's wasn't any real violence...

TED: I think that was our first front page: 'Fans pelt Harvey' in the Melody Maker...

Ian Dickson was the only photographer in the pit at the Manchester Free Trade Hall. 'I remember the hail of debris flying over my head,' he says. 'Alex asked me, have you got your crash helmet with you? But the band were just standing there as bottles and bits of chairs came flying at them, ducking out the way if a bit of metal came at them. I don't know how they stood it... They really were the greatest live band I ever saw. They were very visually striking, and the interplay between them was great. It was a feast for the eyes and the ears.'

Scottish music journalist Billy Sloan first encountered SAHB at this point, at Green's Playhouse (which later became the Apollo). 'They got booed on and cheered off,' he recalls. 'Anybody who looked that gallus *had* to be good. They were the best – bar none.'

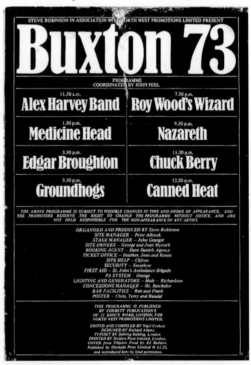

ZAL: Alex instilled in us this idea of being sensational, of aiming to be the greatest band on earth, and that's how we delivered the show. Once you had that attitude it didn't matter who you were supporting, because we were going on to tear the place apart. If the headline band were better than you it didn't matter, because they were supposed to be... But after Slade there were stories about people not wanting us to tour with them because there was that risk. Unless they all just thought we were too crazy... But of course when we went back out six months after Slade the places were full of their fans, saying, we thought you were great but we were at the back of the audience... You could see it panning out – that people would either love us or hate us.

The summer festival season kicked off for SAHB at Buxton – interestingly, the only time they shared a bill with Nazareth. Chuck Berry, Canned Heat and the Edgar Broughton Band were also there, along with Roy Wood's Wizzard, who decided it was too wet to play. Attendees of the show, who revelled in the sonic pleasures of seven 600W speaker towers, had more than the weather to deal with, though – Hells Angels were out for trouble.

The story goes that the Angels made a nuisance of themselves from the early hours, stealing drink and fighting anyone within slipping distance in the muddy field. Once they'd run out of money they began demanding 10p from everyone they met, and even jumped the stage to start raking through performers' pockets while they played. Towards the end of the day, Chuck Berry saw the writing on the wall and began to teach the Angels how to do his trademark walk, patiently demonstrating it again and again until it took him the edge of the stage, at which point he bolted for his car and was gone. It's said he always demanded payment up front.

Alex, meanwhile, turned the opportunity to his advantage.

CHRIS: This big fight kicked off while we were on, and Alex stopped the band. We were so tight he just threw his arms out sideways and, chunk, we all stopped. Then he jumped down into the audience and broke up the fight. It wasn't till a few days later it hit me how badly that could have gone – that was really scary. It could have turned into a riot – you're taking your life in your hands when you do these things.

TED: I saw him watching the Angels from early on. I think he saw the opportunity to do what he was going to do, because it was all about getting attention. He jumped off the stage and started talking to the ringleader as if he was a 12-year-old schoolboy. Later I asked him what he'd said – he'd mentioned the names of a few chapter leaders, and told the guy they wouldn't be happy about him bringing the name of the Angels into disrepute. After that the Angels started coming to all our gigs. Bill was unhappy because he was worried about us becoming a biker band – and we could have done, actually, if we'd stayed on the track Framed had put us on.

But the classic tones of Framed were slipping into the past. Interviewed the week ex-squatmate David Bowie announced he was retiring from music, Alex seems to have been considering the Next situation and how it differed from Framed. 'The last album was a disappointment – at least that's how I see it now,' he said. 'There was a lot of depth and feeling put in but it didn't show because it wasn't produced properly. But we just wanted to get the songs we had down on record. It was a relief to get them down.'

Regarding the Slade tour he commented: 'After that I don't think there's anything we couldn't take on. The reaction we got was electric and it was perfect for us because it was real emotion. Noddy Holder could be one of the most powerful trade union leaders in the country if he felt like it.'

As they began to work on their second album, Alex had decided from early on he wanted to work closely with Hugh, and they were creating material even the most ardent SAHB Angel might have to think twice about.

HUGH: I was always the most qualified musician in any of my bands. I never had to work out drums because Ted has a good ear, but I'd work out the bass part, guitar parts, vocal parts... It made me feel valued – I was helping make things as musical as they could be, and as we all know everyone needs to feel valued.

Alex had all these 40s and 50s influences first-hand but I had them through my parents, and of course I had the music-hall influence too, so I think that's why it made sense to Alex that he and I work together so closely. I don't think he thought I was capable of writing any better than Zal or anyone else – just that I had a bigger bag of tricks.

It was never hard to create but it could be demanding work. There were some very intensive sessions. But in all my time writing with Alex we didn't often struggle for ideas. Sometimes I would take something Zal had had lying about for a while – like on Teenage Idol, that was a riff Zal had come up with in the Tear Gas days. So some things took longer to work out, but it was never arduous.

TED: Hugh's musical ability was like a paintbrush for Alex.

ZAL: He's the musician in the band, the one with a broad range. To a guitar player anyone who plays piano is a real musician – you could ask him to play a minor ninth and he'd play one... Ah, so that's what a minor ninth is... Alex and Hugh would go off together and we'd stay at home and cook. They'd come back and say, we've got a bunch of songs, and we'd add the meat'n'potatoes to try to get a writing credit.

While the work was underway, the band left the confines of the studio to make their first appearance at the Reading Festival. It was to be a historic moment: the sun was setting, the lights came on and 30,000 people's jaws dropped as SAHB unveiled a song they'd written about two weeks previously: The Faith Healer.

ZAL: The whole focus of the day seemed to turn on us. The festival up till then had been the way festivals are, with lots of different things going on, but just at that point, sunset, they brought all the stage lights and the floodlights on, and suddenly the whole place turned round and looked at us.
HUGH: The moment Alex put his hands up in the twin V-sign pose and sang 'Let me put my hands on you', I just knew it was going to be magic. Magic's the only word for it. I had a premonition, the one and only one I've had in my life. As soon as we came off I told the guys, wait till you see the press next week, it's going to be all about us. I was absolutely certain we were going to cop all the press. Rod Stewart was on, Status Quo were on – big big names, but we absolutely slew everybody.
ZAL: It's the band's best-known song and it rolls everything together for me: Alex's creativity and the way Tear Gas wanted to play... it's a masterful song, and playing it for the first time at Reading was magical. The first three songs of the set were where we got them – Faith Healer, Midnight Moses and St Anthony. That's the way it always was with us: this is what we do, if you don't like it you can go home now, and if you stay you're getting more and more of it.

People often ask each other where they were when they heard about JFK, or Princess Diana, or the moon landings. But the first performance of Faith Healer on 25 August 1973 is easier to discuss, because everyone you're talking to knows exactly where you were (Reading) and what you were doing (gaping like a demented hypnotised zombie).

Journalist David Lewis lived through the moment. 'The blatant violence hits an audience in the face, grabbing it by the throat and provoking reaction,' he wrote. Alex told Lewis: 'Reading was like the end of the first phase for us. The Slade tour toughened us up a lot – when we played with them in Glasgow the crowd gave us stick, but it got the adrenalin going. There were three rows flattened and six seats went missing – somebody said they ate them!'

Three weeks later, when SAHB returned to the London Marquee, the word had got out; and, indeed, it seemed as if phase two of the band's media onslaught was underway, with a noticeable change in writers' attitudes. Sounds explained: 'The fact that Harvey is now regarded with a great deal less suspicion than he was previously is in ample evidence. The set opened with a manic version of Crazy Horses which Harvey delivers with a strange menace, the same kind of bitter sweet inflections he seems to inject into everything he does. For the occasion Big Bud's Brass augmented the basic five piece. Their inclusion added a lot of punch, especially on Dance to the Music. Zal Cleminson has become even more pointed and direct in style and pianist Hugh McKenna has improved immeasurably on all counts, the mainstream jazz instrumentals in which McKenna takes all the leads being an excellent example of his understanding. The Harvey Band are undoubtedly among the best live acts currently doing the rounds.'

If anyone needed any further clarification as to how settled, confident and up for it SAHB now were, Next was it. The album was produced by Phil Wainman, who'd developed the glam sound and had been brought in to commercialise SAHB's sound; but if he took some of the terrifying rock edge off the band's noise, he let loose the gigantic creative arc they squeezed into their second LP. Faith Healer had stolen the headlines as a live performance: it was about to do it again as a cult recording. The main feature of the track was the Tootalbug Drone, a strange monolithic rhythmic device invented by Ashton Tootal, the flautist from Hair.

ZAL: Ah, the Tootalbug Drone... I remember going with Alex to get it fixed. Ashton lived in this wee flat in St Albans. His bedroom was like a garage, full of electronic gear all round the walls, and Alex got it fixed, and back came the Drone. Doo–doo–doo–doo–doo–doo... Okay what else can it do? Doo–doo–doo–doo–doo–doo... What about setting three? Doo–doo–doo–doo–doo–doo... Let's go with that one then, shall we?

TED: Alex just wanted something he could play his guitar to – it had foot pedals and you could change the pitch. Nowadays people would use drum machines. He had to dig it out for Next, and after that we used it for the rest of the band's career.

ZAL: Yeah, I wonder why he didn't impose it on us sooner... he must have been planning to!

CHRIS: The reason Faith Healer became cult is the length of the intro. The reason it's so long is we didn't have enough material to properly fill a cassette so Phil stretched the intro out, with Ted's percussion effects speeding down and up. The original intro was about fifteen seconds but Phil turned it into two and a half minutes.

TED: I hated it. I couldn't get what Phil wanted me to do, and I didn't know what was happening. It felt strange. In retrospect it worked – there were lots of interesting ideas. To this day you go into clubs all over the world and you hear it being played. It's a great song, one of the best lyrics Alex wrote.

CHRIS: But Phil had a very clear idea of what he wanted, and you ended up sometimes with a very commercial backing track that didn't work with what we played. LIke with Giddy Up A Ding Dong, you could take off Alex's vocals and put Mud or Sweet over it. You could sing Tiger Feet over it... We did get away with some things, though.

TED: Next was an idea Alex had. I don't know if he'd done it before; but we took a lot of time getting the arrangement. We had to develop and orchestrate it with a rock lineup, make it into something that would carry the lyric. We came up with a big powerful thing. It was our first real heavy statement, the first time we really started to bend things out of shape.

ZAL: It was strange from where we'd come from, trying to use such a small guitar sound and all. Alex's part was everything about it. It was a strange thing for us to be doing, but everyone seemed to think it was a good idea.

Meanwhile, Alex delved into the world of comic-book superheroes for the first time, with an early outing for Vambo. This version, Vambo Marble Eye, was more street gang than crimefighter, but the seeds were sown. The story goes that Alex's son Tyro woke him up in the middle of the night to tell him about a dream he'd had: 'Daddy, I've seen Vambo Marble Eye'. The rest became history – and was to continue doing so.

ZAL: Alex was a real bookophile. He had a marvellous collection of books. He loved the Tarzan books, the Boys' Own type of literature, and he took that into the songs. Good titles, good storylines.

Next is still seen as a classic rock album, a maelstrom of genius arrangements, daring forays from the norm and challenging, demanding originality. Brian Hogg observes: 'The band are very *very* hungry – they've decided they're going to make a go of it. The whole SAHB manifesto is established on that album. Next itself is breathtaking for the power of Alex's delivery. It has the whole spirit of

Ian Dickson

Alex performing Framed
during the Next tour

Brel's original but sounds nothing like it – there's even more menace than Brel. It's almost as if Alex was singing from the viewpoint of the army officer – all that evil, while Brel sings from the point of the sad victim who's had to live through it. And one of the really nice things about SAHB doing Giddy Up A Ding Dong is that the original was by Freddy Bell and the Bellboys, which was the first American rock'n'roll band ever to play in Glasgow.'

ZAL: Giddy Up A Ding Dong? Shite!

If 1972 had ended in a spirit of quiet confidence, 1973 closed with an attitude of superconfidence. In the space of 18 months SAHB had changed from a halfbaked coalition of two nearlys into the next big thing; and transformed from a 'journeyman blues singer' and a group of introverted overplayers into a triumph of performance that quite literally had to be seen to be believed.

ZAL: It was meteoric... One minute there were 100 people coming to see us, then there were 500, then there were 2000 people a night, every night.
EDDIE: They WERE sensational. This is a band that had played thousands of gigs, and a guy who'd had a lifetime of experience in music and theatre. It's brilliant to think about even in retrospect. This band would turn audiences around. People who wanted to kill them would come back and see them. That's talent. One night in a really rowdy venue Alex told the audience to sit down – and they all sat. Total dominance! That's why we're still talking about SAHB today.

Z PERVERSION IS A LAMPPOST IN DISGUISE

ZAL ON NEXT

Though impossible to fully comprehend, SAHB's ability to generate a certain commotion in every village and town at the same time they were recording NEXT was remarkable. It became tribal, like some form of simultaneous dreaming. Z soon realised he should refrain from making errant judgments. So assured was he that when the idea for the white face was adopted he gloried in it, demonstrating his total commitment to this mind-boggling spectacle.

It's a lesson we fail to grasp. Let me be perfectly honest here: no one is intellectually interested in what happens to you when you're shit. If something's shit it's simple, it comes out your arse. Or perhaps we should be fighting with demons over some cliché about intellectual pride. Pride is a universal appropriation, bellows the psychotherapist; all Z remembers telling the psychotherapist is this: 'Would you prefer me to falsify myself, to be a lamppost in disguise, to pander to it? That's what I claim to be perversion. Or to put it another way...

Swampsnake: Now what Alex had in mind here is obviously some form of mild perversion, an antidote to playing table tennis with your chums in the Boys Brigade. Yawning wah-wah sounds good enough to fuckin' eat! The track itself is almost too tight and to be truthful, like much of the album, suffers from a production that's just a little tweedy.

Gang Bang: Popular tune, even with the women. If I were to tell you one thing – admit to one gleeful declaration – it would be this: maybe we should just imagine that life is a promise, a pronounced ideal of spiritual truth. Or better still: why not think of it as a pilgrimage, systematically linking the profane with the sacred? And eventually, with luck, we're all saved...

The Faith Healer: Miracles indeed! And so that's how it was, cruising across a hundred degrees, the glory falling from our mouths, celebrated and unrestrained, each in turn playing host to a carefree ego. We disposed of so many absurdities it was almost criminal. This track sums up SAHB like no other, especially played live.But it was early days, too early to consider what lay beyond the justification.

And *Giddy Up A Ding Dong* is true testament as to just how fallible our sense of reason could be. What was that about shit coming out your arse? Clearly I was wrong...

Next: As any rock guitarist will tell you, playing something like this does indeed turn the knees to jelly... Stimulating and inspired, as a song Next revives the seeds of your own free spirit. It also precludes the notion of SAHB shying away from tackling just about anything.

Vambo Marble Eye: Great lyrical stuff from Alex, stirring up the seeds of Vibrania. Don't you just love living in a lullaby? Wah-wah rools ya bass!

Last of the Teenage Idols: Tenement tantrums all about love – a strange kind of love. Only in a moment of curiosity can you remember it's yourself you're in love with! How utterly brilliant and comical Alex is, with everyone else rocking back and forth behind his frothing, seismic Elvis, shamelessly trying to convince us he's the last of the soft–shoe bananas. Malodorous metaphor, grossly and rampantly delivered with spine–shivering panache. It made Z wonder about the whole process. To envisage oneself at a great feast, absorbing the makeshift moods, belching back at the dunces, at times bemused by the waywardness of fools and neophytes.

And fuck me, it went gold...

3 THE IMPOSSIBLE DREAM

THE BAND deserved a reward for living through the unrelenting grind of 1973, and they got it: three weeks off over Christmas. And then another unrelenting grind; only this year it would be even less relenting and even more grinding. By the close of 1974 SAHB would have left their mark on Europe and the USA, along with recording another two albums – although only one was to be released.

A number of marker events served to demonstrate how far they'd come. In January they played the Nottingham College, which was a promotion from their previous Nottingham appearance at the Boat Club, where Chris nearly died in a 2mph car crush.

CHRIS: The backyard's on a steep angle, so the truck's already there and I'm reversing our car in, and it gets jammed on the angle of the hill. I open my door and half get out to take a look, leaving it in reverse because it's not going anywhere – but Zal and Ted get out to look too, so the car rises and starts moving again. Hugh's still in the back of the car and I'm half way out, but I can't get round the door, I'm having to stagger along with the car, and the truck's looming up. So I shout on Hugh to help and he climbs into the front and hits the accelerator instead of the brake... the car's speeding up, the truck's closer and closer and Hugh's asking me if he's hitting the right pedal! I ended up having to climb onto the roof just as the door got torn off and crushed into the front fender by the truck. I was nearly killed...

In February they presented their Valentine Ball at the sleazy Empire Ballroom on Leicester Square, supported by a sadly forgettable Troggs set. Sounds reported: 'SAHB lurched a little nearer that elusive goal of stardom... I got the impression Alex will try anything – anything – to get the audience off. He's so anarchic, so reckless that you wonder sometimes whether he's not a little deranged. The crowd were like a football crowd: the atmosphere was raucous, talkative and sceptical even of their hero. The Troggs earlier achieved neither perfection or connection and the London Scottish Regiment's pipes and drums only lifted temporarily a mood of confusion and boredom inappropriate to a Valentine's Ball – a mood which was not lifted until the appearance of the definitely Sensational Alex Harvey Band.'

In March they stopped off at Oxford Polytechnic, where fan Mandy Hathway saw them for the third time. 'The last time I'd been ready to soak in the music and everything was going fine until the smoke machine came on – the front rows were engulfed and I swear I can still smell the stuff to this day... So it was good to *see* the band this time! After the show my girlfriends and I trotted round to the back door to see if we could get their autographs, but we were told we couldn't go inside and the door was closed on us. Soon afterwards someone else opened the door, and this

Poster for the Valentine's Ball in 1974

time actually went to tell the boys they had fans waiting. Chris came out and invited us in. Ted offered me some grapes – God knows why I should remember that! – and Alex asked my sister for our phone number. It was a fantastic evening.' A few weeks later Mandy was surprised when Alex actually did call with an invitation to a forthcoming show.

They returned to Scotland in May, visiting Perth, Dundee and Edinburgh, with a homecoming show at the Glasgow Apollo. Alex took the opportunity to underline the band's perception of itself and its value: 'We aren't so much a stage act as a movie,' he told a Daily Record reporter. 'Every take is different – that way we keep our music and ourselves fresh. We've never had a hit – but when we go to America later this year we'll insist on the red carpet at the airport.'

The summer tour also featured a return to Manchester Free Trade Hall and Leeds Town Hall, both of which had played host to the previous year's Slade extravaganza.

CHRIS: That gig at Manchester was the time Graham, Ted's roadie, was crawling towards the drumkit during the show when Zal stepped back, fell over him and tore his jumpsuit all the way up the middle. He got a length of gaffer tape to hold it together but it started peeling off in the heat, and it looked like he had a tail for the rest of the show... When we'd done the encore that night someone jumped onto the stage and grabbed me, so my roadie Dennis ran on to help me. But he overdid it, came on too fast, grabbed the guy and accidentally howked him off the stage into the front rows – who all got out his way so he splatted on the floor. The rest of the audience were like: Yaaaaaay... what? Booooooo! And Alex had missed the lot of it and he was asking, what changed – what happened? But the guy was alright...

Sounds scribe Simon Orrell went to the Leeds show to see how the band had changed. 'Almost a year ago SAHB played to a packed audience of teenyboppers and unnecessarily shocked many of them with their bizarre, over–suggestive and at times degrading act. But this time they showed just how a band can mature in twelve months, both visually and musically. Zal Cleminson is horrific. If he wasn't such a capable musician he would probably be appearing somewhere with Christopher Lee. Harvey puts so much effort into his act yet doesn't seem to break into a sweat. A nice little ditty about his childhood hero, Sergeant Fury, is an experiment that has proved very successful. I wonder now whether the band might try to widen its musical field. Incidentally their stage props are quite good – an old fashioned streetlamp lights up a wall which Harvey duly scrawls on with a can of spray paint – all good stuff.'

A US writer beheld SAHB for the first time over the summer and found the stage show at the prime of its life – even allowing for technical issues. 'Harvey begins his routine with outstretched arms and the band begins to cut in over the backtrack. He sings "Let me put my hands on you" several times – and then real pathos as a technician in shirtsleeves and headphones strides on and stops him mid-sentence. The monitors, he says, are feeding back something cruel. The band go off for some minutes. "Make it look real," says Harvey in an aside. "Just imagine we haven't been on before." They reappear to tumultuous applause and carve back into Faith Healer, Vambo Marble Eye, Sergeant Fury – and the classic Framed which has a brilliant little section where he shoves pieces of the wall in each cheek and delivers his lines in faultless Brando/Godfather style. The fact that they're shithot players hardly comes into it – they conjure up this threatening overcast atmosphere of repressed tension. You feel that at any minute they might leap howling into the front rows brandishing flamethrowers...'

Alex's delivery of Framed was his ultimate character study of violence – mental and emotional as well as physical. The performance showed how deeply he understood his subject, perhaps through his upbringing, perhaps through personal experience, perhaps just because he was fascinated. His character in Framed pretended to be cool, but cool is based on fear; and the undercurrent of angry – not negative – energy during the rest of the show could be seen as a function of genuine anarchy – the positive intellectual kind – rather than hatred.

His dad was, if anything, a stronger character than Alex; Eddie Tobin notes you could have had two Alex Harvey Bands if the father had gone into music too. And this strong influential character had been a conscientious objector at a time when it required a lot of guts to do it. Alex had objected too but it was slightly easier in his time.

And Alex preached pacifism and peace: 'Don't make any bullets, don't buy any bullets, don't shoot any bullets – because when you do, you only make a rich man richer'. And yet he was well capable of the odd Glesga Kiss when it was required. He was fascinated by military history and had a huge collection of toy soldiers. It seems almost as if Alex had learned something essential about violence, and therefore the human condition, that he wanted to tell the world – if we could only understand.

The theme of violence followed SAHB right through the 70s. A lot of that may be to do with the English–based press' perception of a hard–nut Glasgow rock band, but SAHB's performances discussed, toyed with and lectured over the issue through set-pieces.

In mid-1974 Melody Maker's Allan Jones discussed the band and violence. Allan, who once said SAHB were the only band who made any kind of sense to him, was such a fan that he hitch-hiked to every gig he could make. That summer Alex told him: 'The most violent people I've ever met had the warmest hearts. They were really emotional. If that energy was directed into a different channel, you're gonna get something that's good. The world floating through space is a bit like a lifeboat. Unless men start thinking about it, and understanding it, they've got to realise they can't have it. But I'm very optimistic and so are the kids I meet. We don't get any wrecked places – to incite people to wreck a place is easy – it's too easy. People ask me about violence as if I was some sort of expert. All I've got to say is, violence is a waste of energy which could be used in other ways.' During the same interview Alex touched on the notion of himself as a leader, discounting it completely: 'I can't help the band by leading them. All I can do is set some kind of example. Leaders haven't got anything.'

ZAL: Underneath, Alex was in a rage all the time – he was angry for all kinds of reasons. So when SAHB came along it gave him a platform to state his case, and he used it. But I remember one night in a club, some guy kept getting in Trudy's way and Alex just stuck the heid on him – bang, it was over, and the rest of the band started dancing round with Alex to make sure it didn't go any further. The guy got dragged off and that was it. Alex was a survivor – he looked after number one. And he never explained himself that way to the band. We didn't need to be intellectual about it – it was wrapped up in rock'n'roll and that's what we were there for.

Violence and pacifism, rage and reflection, leadership and example, socialism and selfishness... There's a truth somewhere in there, hidden so deep it's beyond the scope of a rock biography. Well, this one anyway.

THE rollercoaster of write-rehearse-gig-record went on, and in the middle of it five individuals tried to keep their lives together. Friends were made on the road, relationships were built among companions, and characters were frayed at the edges.

DAVE: There was a nucleus of people we saw at every gig, and it was incredible how far they would travel... but there wasn't a bunch of hangers–on. The band hung about together. We saw some of Alex's close friends from time to time but they were never part of the whole band thing. Still, it was nice to see friendly faces wherever you went.

CHRIS: Wives and girlfriends is always a sticky thing for bands. We realised was it was better to bring them all out together for a while instead of one at a time, because if you only had one wife there the other half stopped being a member of the band during her visit. That's not to take anything away from anyone's wife, far from it. But when the band goes somewhere after a gig and he doesn't go, he's thinking, what are they up to? What are they talking about? What are they saying about me?

TED: A lot of the ideas and inspiration a band gets comes from the time they spend together, so it's crucial not to miss out if you want to be part of the creative process.

CHRIS: And by being careful about it you avoided the situation of wives falling out – oh, why was she there and I wasn't, and all that. Another thing you have to be careful about is taking sides – if someone doesn't understand the situation it can get out of hand. I mean, say for example, Ted's in a bad mood. Now, it may well be Ted's fault – it probably is – but I have to say, my drummer's in a bad mood, it's affecting his game, and I have to blame the girlfriend. I have to. It's wrong, but welcome to the real world... These are the kind of things that bring a band down if you don't watch it.

Meanwhile, Hugh was beginning to lose his grip on the rock'n'roll lifestyle...

CHRIS: We'd hired a a big expensive colour telly for our flat, and all seven of us were sitting watching it, and Hugh got up and turned the colour right down because it was messing with his head...

He discussed it with us, and it wasn't like he was hearing voices, but he knew something wasn't right... and at no point did anyone say, this is too difficult, get him to fuck; we were all wanting to know if there was any way we could help.

He accused Ted and I of being freemasons. Never mind anything else, but how we could have found time to become freemasons without Hugh knowing about it, I'll never know... The doctor came in and put him under sedation, told us it was just a bit of stress, and next morning Hugh came down and quite naturally said, sorry I accused you of being masons, I now know that was rubbish – you're not masons. And in the next breath he said, you're all fuckin' *foresters*. What the fuck is a forester? That story got a life of its own...

HUGH: That became a joke later on – when we played in Aberdeen we'd pass a place called Temple of Fiddes and Chris would say, Hey Hugh – that's where all us foresters meet, with the Grand Oak Leaf and all that...

THE band's summer season included two big festival shows, of which the Bucolic Frolic at Knebworth was the first. SAHB shared the stage with the Allman Brothers, Van Morrison, the Doobie Brothers and Tim Buckley. The Mahavishnu Orchestra arrived in five white Ford Cortinas, each driven by a chauffeur dressed all in white, and a band member climbed out each car dressed in a white kaftan.

CHRIS: I've never laughed so much in my life! Then we had the argument with the Doobie Brothers. They'd got the wrong dressing room and they were in ours, so Alex and I went in and gave it the Glaswegian, this is *oor* fuckin' dressin' room... So they said, are you the Alex Harvey Band? We went, fuckin' aye. They went, We're leaving! That's all it was, there wasn't any knife action or any of

Barry McCulloch

SAHB seen from the cheap seats at Knebworth: the green blob centre-stage can only be Zal

the stories people tell you. It was very amicable, up to a point...

I had terrible sunburn on my back – I had to be all bandaged up so I could wear the bass. There were about 120,000 people there, I walked on with my shoulder killing me, went to the front of the stage to start Faith Healer and my curly lead came out the amp and fired away into the air in front of me... So I start yanking it back in, but meanwhile Tam's done the clever thing. He's got another lead, plugged it into the amp and he's come up and put the other end in the bass. I don't notice he's done that, so I get the curly lead and put it back in the amp, thinking it's still plugged into my bass... nothing! Fuckin' curly leads...

Festival warrior 'gwshark' was in the audience at Knebworth and remembers the SAHB set. 'Alex announced: "Today our new single came out, which is why they're having this festival. It's true, you know..." Then they launched into Sergeant Fury, with the chorus about wanting to be rich and famous – I guess from his attitude he didn't really want that anyway! Then during Dance To The Music he said, "Don't piss in the water supply, because it's your bottle and we all live in it".'

Ex-pat Barry McCulloch, born in Falkirk but habite en Australia, went along to see the Allmans and the Doobies. 'I'd never heard of SAHB. We had just finished a nice big joint when they came on, and I loved them from the start. I took a photo of them on stage from miles away – but you can tell the tiny green blob in the middle is Zal! To me they were the highlight of a great festival. When I got back to Australia I got the band I was in to do Giddy Up A Ding Dong, and we attempted Last of the Teenage Idols too.'

CHRIS: As I was leaving in my big Cadillac, the passenger door opens and this guys appears, sits down and says: 'It's a long road, and no one knows where it's going...' Well, I said, I know where *you're* going – get ti' fuck!

The impossible album: promo artwork for the abandoned album, which made it into the press

Lindsey McF

Above, fan snaps of the band before and during a show in the Impossible Dream tour of 1974; and, left, an early limited-edition cloth patch

The second big show was a triumphant return to Reading – a year after they'd blown everyone away they headlined the first day of the festival. Photographer Ian Dickson remembers: 'When the pipers came on for Anthem I had tears in my eyes – it always works for Scots abroad... misguided national loyalty!'

October saw the release of The Impossible Dream, the band's third official studio album; but in fact it was the fourth. The LP had originally been called Can't Get Enough, and an advertising campaign had even been completed for the title. But producer Shel Tamby's attempts at commercialising the SAHB sound had resulted in such a poor showing the tapes were destroyed.

ZAL: There we were again, trying to bring in someone who could create hip music. I got the impression when we were introduced to Shel that he was on the way down... It was like, yeah, I remember him, he's done the Who and the Kinks and that, but what's he up to now? His whole approach was laid-back and dozy – I kept thinking he was asleep. Maybe he was listening, but it looked like he was asleep. Something was just not working. SAHB didn't really do overdubs – we had the arrangement and we played the songs so often we didn't need to practice all that much. But Shel was like, can you do another take, can you try this, can you add that – and that's just not the way we worked. We thought, this is how it sounds, you should be capturing that. So it was all dull and muffled – there was no energy or life in it.

CHRIS: It was Bill's idea – because Phil Wainman wasn't available, he got Shel Tamby. We'd always humour Bill – I don't mean in a bad way. We'd run it up the flagpole and see who saluted it, but if it came to the point it wasn't working we said so. So Bill got Shel in and said, don't worry, it won't be shite, this guy's the master of the mix... and after listening to the second track he's like, naw, you're right – it didn't work. By the way, Hugh Padgam was the teaboy on the Shel sessions... now he's world famous in his own right!

The only solution was to record the album again – and this time old hand Dave Batchelor took the chair. With his inside knowledge of the band, from running the live sound to having spent years drinking with them, he had the right experience and right talent to make it work. Alex said, 'We were all sitting in the same car going to gigs, staying in the same hotel, and that's why Davie was perfect. He was there while the songs were constructed – and that's when the hard work's done.'

CHRIS: Impossibly, it went like a dream for once. And the dance to Sergeant Fury – it was great.

HUGH: And it's nice to have a dance to that because it goes with the Vaudeville feel. I was able to bring in the music-hall influences I'd got from my parents, which is something very few rock bands had access to. Alex had been scratching around for an idea and I hadn't come up with anything for ages because I'd been ill. Alex went, you haven't said anything for about three months... And I said, it's kinda difficult when you're trying to piece your personality back together. He said, aye well, I'm trying to get an idea for this song... and rather timorously I suggested the Vaudeville tune – he liked it, and we built the song round it.

CHRIS: Gang Bang was fun too – there was no political correctness at the time. It was all good fun. I always noticed when we stopped the music for people to sing along, it was all women's voices you heard. It wasn't controversial in the context of SAHB. I mean, you can't just put it on in a pub but if it was a SAHB night you could, because then it's just another SAHB song that's good fun.

HUGH: I always had a slight problem with Gang Bang because of the lyrics, but I know it's tongue in cheek. I like the music though. I didn't refuse to do it – I didn't know any better at the time!

TED: And of course Alex re–visited Vambo. The original Vambo was more gang–related in

Harvey–speke. It was Glaswegian gang stuff and the characters all had gang nicknames. But he developed the character and second time around he'd become more of a superhero with a vision of a better life for everyone. There were a couple of themes that were part of the band's sense of humour, that were used again and again for inspiration.

CHRIS: And Rolling Stone said the outro, Hey Is That You Pissing Down My Leg, was Alex using his jazz voice. They said it showed he could sing when he wanted to... but it's me singing!

Charles Shaar Murray called it 'the first rock and roll comic book. Populated with thumbnail–sketch characterisations, splashy musical primary colours and a peculiar kind of verbal shorthand, The Impossible Dream validates the trash ethic with triumphant ease. Which means it's one mo-fo of a rock and roll album.' Murray enthused about the band being even better live than the album made them sound, citing The Man in the Jar as one track which defined them as a first division act.

But despite a healthy chart entry, The Impossible Dream didn't satisfy Mountain's requirements for a big hit. The battle of business versus art was set to continue through the band's career, and neither party was ever fully satisfied.

TED: You had to get a hit single and then the albums would sell. I think the management had a headache – how do you condense what this band is about into one song? It was difficult to find something simplistic enough that could do the job. We didn't really care, though – we were selling out constantly. They misunderstood that and they didn't think we could do the commercial thing.

Mandy Hathway

ZAL: That funny word, commercial... Be commercial... We were successful on the road and we were building a fanbase. But we weren't supposed to just be the band we were – we were meant to aim for Top of the Pops and stuff. We tried writing stuff like Jungle Jenny, I Wanna Have You Back... but it's just contrived. What's in the charts? Let's come up with that... And you can hear Alex trying to come down off his blues and soul-based delivery and join this teeny-bop idiom. Sometimes it works, sometimes it just makes your toes curl.

TED: I remember Alex talking about having to unlearn singing in an American accent. People loved the way he'd sing in a Scottish accent, loved or hated. He always felt the pressure was for him to be a certain way as opposed to be who he was. The honesty was important to him and that was one of the battles he kept having, Bill would say, maybe if you wore

Alex tries the pipes on UK tour in 1974

this, got your hair like this... He didn't want to conform to being anyone else.

ZAL: The gigs were fantastic – everywhere we went crowds were getting bigger and bigger. But we didn't equate that to not shifting units. The industry was very wary of Alex. Your mum couldn't sing along to us – he wasn't exactly tuneful. But that was Alex... we accepted that, the kids at the shows did too, and we blew people away and that's what was important to us. Alex was ambivalent about it too – everyone could see we were big. But it must have been a frustration for some people.

CHRIS: So then – get this – they got other people to write songs for us! Hot Chocolate wrote one for us and Jeff Beck produced it. It must exist out there but you don't want to find it: 'A hungry man must eat, a sleepy man must sleep, but when I am in love I want to make love...' And Pete Brown wrote Dead End Kids for us: 'Dead end kids you're on the skids, dead end boys you've got no toys...' He's thinking that's Alex's kinda lyric. Fuck off.

A US promo image from 1974 showing Alex, the band and pipers

AFTER yet another series of UK dates, SAHB headed to Europe with Deep Purple. The most memorable moments from the trip are the band having to pee on the truck's wheels to free it from ice, and a mooning competition between the Purple and SAHB tour buses – which SAHB won when backing singer Vicki Silva flashed her assets.

Then immediately afterwards, in November, the band left for their first foray to the USA. They had press receptions in New York, Boston and Philadelphia and took in Los Angeles, Phoenix, Dallas, Chicago, Cleveland, Detroit and Northampton, among others. The visit included the first-ever live broadcast by NY radio station WQIV FM from Electric Ladyland – an experiment in quadraphonic production. And SAHB played a week-long residency in the LA Whiskey Bar.

ZAL: Being in New York, being in Electric Ladyland... it was like, wow. It was a bit like when we came from Glasgow to London. This is great – things happen here. Then getting to New York was exactly the same buzz: so much has happened here musically.

TED: The Gallowa' Hills hit me again – it's all about leaving and going to America – 'come with me and share my love in a far country'. And I remember early on my first morning in New York, walking down Seventh Avenue and thinking: this is me, on the other side of the Gallowa' Hills... The bookers told us they'd wanted us because so many people had seen our In Concert show, recorded at the Rainbow, and they'd hated us – we were upsetting people without even being in the country!

DAVE: The big problem was that when we were supporting people we had half-hour slots; it was very difficult to put across what the band were about in half an hour. But when the pipers came on for Anthem, that made a connection with the Americans. It was well worth it.

CHRIS: We had to fight to get the pipers on the tour, but in the end we had three guys to pick from so we had two every night. Tim McCabe was one – I remember one night he was in the hotel swimming pool. The whole band and the crew jumped in to give him a ducking, and he ducked every single one of us – that's when we realised he wasn't bullshitting about having been in the Marines. Seven against one and he wiped us out!

Then when we played with Aerosmith they had a huge PA system, all painted white, and Alex sprayed 'Vambo' on it and they went fuckin' ape–shit! I don't think they remember about that – I don't think they were quite 'there' at the time. There's a rumour when they were in the UK Steven Tyler gave someone $6000 to buy them smack, and the guy did a runner and spent the $6000 – I mean, what was Tyler gonny do, sue?

ZAL: A lot of people were just baffled – but in New York, Cleveland, LA, where people were into things that were a bit different, they got it and they liked it. But anywhere in between we had a problem. It was difficult playing the big stadiums – you can't get the intimacy, you can't get the theatre. If you rolled it forward a few years, big screens and music videos, we could have ripped the arse out of it.

When they headed for home a few days before Christmas, the job was done and The Impossible Dream was in the US Top 100; and the band had generated enough interest to come back again soon and continue the age-old battle of breaking the States.

Lee Hagan

SAHB Stateside: Top pictures, Alex and Zal during Man In The Jar; bottom two, during Next; right, Midnight Moses

Z PROUD WITHOUT BRAGGING

ZAL ON THE IMPOSSIBLE DREAM

In Z's beginning you will remember he was adrift beneath the courtly light of the five moons, in a world collectively known as Hail Vibrania, with the imprint of madness straining irresistibly to halt everything in its tracks. And then, just as he'd grown into the habit of unsettling his life by ignoring Gorbal's advice about masturbating in public, SAHB's willing desire to plant something vaguely tyrannical emerged.

The Hot City Symphony: With the smell of oily steel riffs, pit–pony drumming and wooden icons, Alex manages to rearrange our frenzied heads with this monumental offering. Unlike Vambo, we were merely a vibrant collection of elemental little insects, morbidly thrashing out an uninhibited truth. It was just what Alex had dreamed of: a hero all to himself.

Vambo started out as a demo with Jeff Beck producing. For some reason he freaked out at the band's sheer intensity and decided instead to jam around some Stevie Wonder stuff with us. Halfway through Z burst a string and decided instead it was time to sit back, get shit–faced and admire one of his all-time heroes.

The Man the the Jar! it read, pasted on a high billboard above the tunnel to the prison. The Man In The Jar! TV chat show! Live at the theatre! Tonight's guest... The Faithhealer.

'Is that Mr Faithhealer or just Faithhealer? You're not The Sensational Faithhealer or anything like that, are you?'

'No – that's someone else, a kind of tribute Faithhealer, I suppose. An impostor.'

'Just introduce him as The Faithhealer, okay? Just th-eee Faithhealer.'

'Th-eeee Faithhealer it is.'

'Pronounced "The Man In The Jar."'

Then came his catchphrase. 'Stay with the power, cry money! Tourists in a world of pain! Cry money, from the test tube to the grave! Cry money!' Someone screamed like a baby. Up went the lights and out went the need for anything but mindless TV.

'Get me a sponge – I just love this,' said the Impregnator, dusting himself off.

'What the fuck do you mean?' said the Man in the Jar. 'When you set out to make such an impact, half alive and half mental, you must have thought the wisdom of the world was with you?'

The Faithhealer bent forward as if he had an ulcer and grimaced, tough–guy style. 'Sorry, I don't ever remember being that perceptive.'

'*On air in five...*'

The falsetto voices of the beginners in the audience suddenly battered into his head.

'So this is being famous,' he thought.

'You misunderstand me,' the Man in the Jar said.

'Tricky this, isn't it?' Whispered the Faithhealer. 'Never believe anything that conditions your mind to behave as though you have an ego.'

'Oh! That may be difficult – you see, I'm a paranoid schizophrenic,' The Man in the Jar stated. He looked at the crowd then snatched a test smile at the camera. 'I'm more interested in Tomorrow Belongs To Me,' he whispered. 'By the way, you're not a Nazi, are you?'

'Listen, you turd, if I were a diving bird, and all the world was a sea of ghostly waves, and I could swoop long enough to divert my attention away from my purpose and swoop again into the falling foam to capture just *one moment* of truth from your mouth, you dilapidated, predacious fuckin' nailbrush —'

'Okay! We'll be right back after this break. Don't go fingering your favourite gal!' The Man in the Jar swept out the studio to the sound of distant cheering...

River of Love: Game excuse for a pop song. Check out Magnus the Swede's version – great!

Long Hair Music: What starts out as a pastiche suddenly gets terribly serious and, with a little bit of dressing, could have been a contender. Repetitive lyric is just Alex getting bored with reiterating the theme of shagging something. This time it's cherry pie!

Hey... Is That You Pissing On My Leg: Glen Benson, the housewives' favourite.

Sgt Fury: I'm not sure if I really like this sort of thing. And if the two remaining Tear Gas fans, now contemplating suicide, still hated Alex that much, this is all it needed to start them hacking at their wrists.

Weights Made of Lead: Compliant blarney.

Money Honey/Impossible Dream: Now I can think about it dispassionately, what's the point of dragging yourself all the way to Vibrania to end up pissing in the wind with this crap?

The Tomahawk Kid: He switched on the TV and watched someone hoovering and then something having sex; someone teaching Vibranian and then someone delivering a quantum cause for the crucifixion. He heard people laughing; laughing at all of this, from gasping, unmerciful corridors and beyond... The Kid felt his eyes balloon from his head, as the rope stiffened around his neck. He heard nothing of the snap – and nothing of his last breath. By the time the patrols arrived the harbour house had been emptied. A service lift brought his body up from the cellar and it lay at the back of a small room, draped in his favourite fur coat. Soon the room filled with a strong–smelling dust, as the body was first sprayed and then sealed. It lay covered like the purple pupa of an enormous moth, completely surrounded by a thick gel.

Anthem: In a circle of friends, within the space of a single song, Alex grapples with the opinions of his forebears. From a limpy–legged fool dragged through the ritual of supply and demand, he manages, in the end, to commit the afflictions of a whole nation to history... And in a way SAHB was born! Somehow, after cringing about sleeping seven to a room, the idea of being sensational, of showing off gleefully, suddenly reminded us how to be proud without bragging about it.

4 TOMORROW BELONGS TO ME

STATISTICALLY 1975 was the band's biggest year. They became the biggest-grossing live act in the UK and experienced their highest-ever chart placing. Both achievements came about for the same reason: they spent almost the entire year on the road, clocking up over 100 dates in nine months. That's nearly a gig every two days from March til December – and doesn't make any allowance for time spent writing, rehearsing, recording or sleeping.

The first US tour of the year was in the company of The Tubes, with the bands taking turns headlining depending on popularity – in Cleveland, for example, SAHB sold more records than Elton John that year. Tubes' backing singer and dancer Le Roy Jones recalls being surprised the two bands got on: 'I loved SAHB's show but I think Alex thought we were a big-budget act at first,' he says. 'Once he realised we created everything ourselves and got very little support he reacted differently. The Tubes didn't have that much in common with SAHB – they were hard Glasgow and we were young, rich white Utopia nightmares... but when he saw us doing White Punks on Dope, our take-off of British rock stars, he really got it.'

Alex took their new relationship to the extreme, as ever, marching onto the stage during their set with the pipers, singing The Gallowa' Hills and stopping the show in its tracks. The overdressed overblown Tubes loved it. The pipers trick became a standard Harvey sketch wherever the band went.

TED: It didn't matter – all we needed was the pipers and as many of us as we could muster. When we were rehearsing in SIR in New York, Dylan, Baez and Ronson were using it. So we all got into the freight lift and went up and down singing the Gallowa' Hills, pipes blaring, feet stamping, making a right fuckin' racket. Alex said, these fuckers'll never forget us! Then we were staying in a Holiday Inn somewhere and there was a house band playing away in the corner of the cocktail bar. Alex marshalled us together, got the pipers ready and we stamped through The Gallowa' Hills again... Everyone fuckin' loved it – it was drinks on the house!

CHRIS: We were playing the Palladium in New York, and there's three or four Arnold Schwarzenegger types in the front row, muscles rippling, and they all had these t–shirts on with 'MY GAL ZAL' written on them! Zal's just like, aaaaw, fuck's sake... He had to have heavy security coming off, he was shitting himself! These guys where huge – don't shoot them, you'll only upset them...

ZAL: They tried to jump in the limousine: 'Come on, Zal, we're going to a party!' No we're not.

Fan Todd Miller remembers more or less having given up hope of ever seeing SAHB. 'We somehow found out they were playing in Chicago with the Tubes. The marketing line was, if this is not the most outrageous show you have ever seen, you can ask for a refund. The gig wasn't crowded but the guys were outstanding, so we moved up to the second row and I seem to remember we stood out as far as our enthusiasm for the show... But then the Tubes came out – talk about going from amazing to awful in twenty minutes! We went to the ticket window, told them it was not the most outrageous show we'd ever seen, got a full refund and happily drove home back to Bloomington, Illinois.'

CHRIS: There were all these silly games we played at airports... We had this game, RugWatch, where you had to try to spot wigs. Zal was shite at it. I'd quietly say: three o'clock, forty feet away, syrup... But he'd see someone right up close, and start pointing at them shouting: Wig! *Wig!* **Wig!**
　　Alex had a great thing for when the Mormons and that started hassling you. He bought this huge Bible, the weight of two engineering bricks, and he carried it about with him. And in his bag he had this fuckin' awful smelly cheese – this stuff had a half–life. Whenever he saw Mormons or Adventists or whatever he'd go, you're just the guy I want to talk to... He'd eat some of the cheese and start quoting from his Bible at them with his garbage–breath. They're like, no it's fine, and Alex would start chasing them round the airport. Of course when we got on the plane Alex had a row to himself – the stink was mingin'...

A photo around this time shows the band lined up in front of their aircraft, each happily holding a paper bag like a purse. Each bag contained a stack of hash cakes – but by the time they settled in the plane, someone had managed to eat their way through the lot. Identifying the culprit was simply a case of waiting until the guilty party blurted out: 'Oh man, the colours on the seat are too much!' and promptly went Zal-white.

Zal himself had a similar escapade in another US airport, overdoing the recreational substances until he no longer needed makeup. Chris tried rushing him to the toilet but they only made it as far as the balcony, from where Zal projectile-vomited on a passing group of businessmen below. Then they did a runner.

SAHB's US publicist, Barbara Birdfeather, enthused about life on the road with the guys in a cleaned-up article for the fan club.

Seven-thirty a.m. – an ungodly hour at best, made unnaturally uncomfortable by the incessant ringing of the bedside telephone. Eyes barely opening, I grope for the phone, slowly realising I'm in the Holiday Inn of the city where the Sensational Alex Harvey Band is playing tonight. It's a call from London, someone inquiring whether they could do a phone interview with Alex later that day. Relieved it wasn't a major catastrophe, we arrange a mutually convenient time, mutter pleasantries about the weather and hang up.

I turn over, then sit up, unable to get back to sleep. The excitement of the upcoming gig is already getting to me. A headline date in an industrial, middle American town wouldn't normally seem important, but this is a place that is just crackers over the band — SAHB sells more records here than the States' top record seller, Elton John; gigs are sold out just about as soon as they're announced; the kids occasionally spray 'Vambo Rools!!' on back street walls. You had to know tonight was gonna be something special!

Grab a fast breakfast, thoughts racing – get the final touches together, make sure everything works, make the difference between a good gig and a great one. Joining me were Dick O'Dell, tall, blonde, tour manager and Dave Batchelor, sound man and album producer for SAHB since its inception.

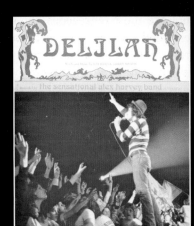

Above left, ticket to Billy Connolly's party in January 1975; above right, Delilah sheet music

dear boys & girls,

As we start on our British tour — be good, don't smash any windows or throw any rubbish. We look forward to seeing you because we love you & that's why we don't want you to get into any trouble.

love
XXXXX ALEX

Left, a 1975 tour badge; above, Alex's message to fans in the tour programme

Above: Chris, Zal and Alex performing Delilah on TV, with Hugh in the background to the lef

The Sensational
ALEX HARVEY BAND

CHRISTMAS
SHOW 1975

Official Programme

23 *The Sensational*
ALEX HARVEY BAND 23

Christmas Show. 1975

VIP GUEST

Access to Hospitality Room only

Name _____ Hugh McKenna

JSE _____ Trevor Perry _____ MM _____

GREETINGS TELEGRAM *

T30 TGMS HD117 APG 1013 LONDON T 22
                    ALLPURPOSE

MR HUGH MCKENNA 9 GREEN LANE CLOSE
BYFLEET SURREY

    WE ARE 21 TODAY - LOOKING FORWARD TO NUMBER 1 STOP
    CONGRATULATIONS
                    BILL

Far left, the
Christmas tour
programme
above, a gig's
backstage pass
left, telegram
from Bill to
Hugh marking
Live's char
entry in 197

More brief discussion – 'Do those front monitors really work?' – slurps of coffee, echoes of 'see ya la-ta,' and we were all off, not to see each other til early evening. Up to the room, endless phone calls to the outside world all day. A look in the mirror, check my bag for stickers, the extra pen and the backstage list, a last call from the Atlantic Records promotion man assuring me everything's just swell, and down to the lobby where the band is slowly assembling to go to the sound check for the gig.

HIT THE ROAD! Ted McKenna is down first, tuxedo in one hand, the other raised in a gentle wave. Hugh McKenna, Ted's keyboard cousin, wanders in. 'Have ya seen ma new shades?' he says, posing a bit. The lobby light catches the navy glass, making it seem for a moment that Hugh really does have stars in his eyes. The Gas guys, zippo guitarist Zal Cleminson and Scorpio bassist Chris Glen, are next, carrying stage gear in cases, wearing long silky white scarves and oh-so-tight blue jeans, with Alex himself, looking somewhat sleepy and definitely dishevelled, in the rear.

'Wot time is it?' Alex yawns.

'Time to go – into the limos.' It's tour manager Dick O'Dell, ushering us into the waiting autos, motors running. Doors slam, and we're off to the gig.

The hall is cool and draughty, cables crossing the stage busy with roadies as SAHB members pick their way to the amps and plug in. A few tentative chords at first. Ted picks up the tempo and leads the way through a funky jam. Alex, cigarette in one hand, beer in the other, does a 'Test, test' through the mike he'll be storming songs through in just a few hours.

The sound check over, it's off to the dressing rooms for a bite to eat and the spectacle of Alex and Chris exercising, kind of slow motion kung fu that seems to involve Bruce Lee imitations! The stark walls echo with roars of laughter and encouragement to the semi-Samurai Scottish warriors. Our clowning about ends, though, when diligent Dick swings the door open with, 'Thirty minutes! Get yer makeup on, Zal!'

I exit, check out the crowds (excited, they're bubbling with anticipation), and the burly security dude stationed at the back door, and find myself a place among the large speakers at stage left. Just enough time for one last cigarette and...

Houselights off. The vibrating pulsing electronics of 'Fanfare' as spotlights sweep the audience, and suddenly there he is.

HIT THE STAGE! 'Good evenin' boys and gurrls' — Alex in inevitable striped vest, pirate jacket and well worn jeans. 'It's lovely to be here tonight and I'd like to introduce you to ma band, the Sensational Alex Harvey Band!'

The crowd noise becomes deafening, the intro to Faith Healer heard over the wild applause as Ted, Hugh, Zal and Chris take their places, pick up "Faith Healer's" mesmerising beat – and they're off. At an almost dizzying pace SAHB virtually tear through their set. Before the frenzied applause for "Faith Healer" has a chance to die down, Midnight Moses (with Zal, Alex and Chris leering over the stage monitors) takes us on that wild ride. Cries for Vambo ring through the hall and sure enough, Alex whips up to the mike with the thick black Vambo book held high.

'This is a tale of two cities ... my city and YOUR city.' Snap. The book slams shut, house lights out and Ted's tom-tom beats in time to the hearts pounding and kids shouting right along and right through Hot City Symphony. Whew! Before anyone can recover we get Delilah, Gamblin' Bar Room Blues, the epic Framed, and finally Anthem.

The slow and pompous strains reach through the hall. 'If you don't put me on trial, then why don't you turn me loose?' Alex pleads and the kids respond. When he raises his arms *high, fingers in the victory V, they do so too, standing unhesitatingly and swaying in rhythm, the dance of ages. The pipers march stately on stage, their minor harmonies blending beautifully with the electricity of SAHB's majestic music.*

All too soon it's over. SAHB bow in smiling unison and leave the stage to thunderous applause, returning to rip through Gang Bang and Jumping Jack Flash for an encore. Exhausted but beamingly happy, they file off.

HIT THE BOTTLE! Back in the dressing room it's cheerful chaos. Alex whooshes open a beer can that explodes its foamy contents not only over himself, but gives Chris and Dick a thorough soaking as well. The pipers are divesting themselves of their woollen uniforms while Zal cold–creams his makeup off. Outside press and radio people are eager to say hello to the band, and after giving the lads a chance to 'get decent' I usher them in. Gushing groupies look on adoringly, but as always their chances with the SAHB are nil.

Slowly the band winds down. The last of the goodies are eaten, stage gear is safely tucked in cases, glances between the assembled company indicate it's time to take our leave of this place that's been so good to us. Back into the shiny limos, back to the Holiday Inn.

In the hotel lobby nobody notices us. Sure there are glances at the strange gear and all, but SAHB are not the heroes they were just a few minutes ago. That's OK though, 'cuz we know that the band brought a little Scottish magic to the sons and daughters of some of these very people. Alex made their kids happy.

CHRIS: When we came home we landed at Heathrow. I'm coming down the stairs and Alex is at the bottom near these three cleaning ladies, who are wondering if they recognise me because of this brilliant tigerskin jacket I'm wearing. And Alex goes, you must remember him – he's Glen Benson. Remember? The housewife's dream, they called him? They're going, I think I remember the name... Alex says, yeah, don't you remember his big Number One? The Dreams My Heart Can Build? So I get to the bottom of the stairs and they put down their cleaning machines and ask for my autograph. And Alex is grinning his head off – gotcha!

At last there was a break in the gigging schedule – but only to work on their fourth album. By now the creative process had been honed down and work went smoothly. The result was Tomorrow Belongs To Me, featuring a daring rip-off of the title track, perceived as a Nazi anthem.

CHRIS: Alex gave us free reign to bring musical ideas in, then he'd say yea or nay to them. If he liked something he'd open the big book with stickers and bits of cheese and chewing gum all over it, and find a lyric that would work with the music. Or he'd say, listen, I need a bit of blues, and we'd play about til we were doing something he liked. He'd chip in with arrangements and that but the music mainly came from us. There was stuff like Stone Eater, ten songs in one, that disappears up its own arse. But it was great fun to play.

Making things up off the cuff was always fun too – that's how we wrote Ribs and Balls. It's about that thing where you start taking the order for the Chinese and by the time you get to the fifth guy the first guy says, yeah, I want that instead... so we said, fuck it, five portions of ribs, five portions of balls, and that solved it for ever after.

HUGH: Chef was a very intense job. It worked well though. It was worth it.

Fan Michael Hightower recalls running into Tomorrow by accident. 'I couldn't stop listening to it – the strength of the performances, combined with Alex Harvey's impossibly strange and powerful voice; Zal Cleminson's balls–out guitar; and the loopy arrangements of completely unexpected songs hooked me.'

The epic ambitions of Chef and Stone Eater are reflected in some of Alex's comments in the press around the same time. Perhaps it was that he'd turned 40 that February, but there was a little more lecturing than usual in his interviews.

'Suddenly, freedom is hard to get,' he told the Glasgow Herald. 'I'm losing touch with what gave me the first trigger to get on in this business. 'I think I might make a real attempt to retrace the footsteps of my youth – I might take a tent and spend some time camping around the Highlands. I'll go alone – I need some time to think.'

He told Simon Clarke in Disc he didn't find any other musician particularly influential any more. 'I can admire a group like the Bay City Rollers and I can even admire a punk group that can't even play – as long as they believe in what they are doing.

'People have said to me I should have made it a long time ago,' he went on. 'I don't really know what they mean. Made what? Maybe made a hit single? Maybe I'd have been a big star in 1963 or something. But maybe I'd have cracked up in 1964.'

WITH just four days off, SAHB began another UK tour, which was to be immediately followed by another US outing, this time supporting Jethro Tull. The band's position at home was secured, with many dates selling out three weeks in advance. The tour also included two stadium supports with Yes (tickets £2.50).

CHRIS: The Birmingham Odeon was a steep hall running down the stage, which wasn't raised because with the angled chairs it didn't need to be. Near the end of the show this guy grabbed about a dozen t–shirts from the merchandise stall and started throwing them into the audience as he took a runny onto the stage. It was the time of the show where Alex had two or three people up anyway, so he just welcomed the guy onstage and put his arm round him, and the security guys were fizzing... Later on I found out John Taylor, who would end up in Duran Duran, dogged school to get my autograph at the soundcheck that day. It turns out Andy Taylor did the same thing at Newcastle once.

Fan and photographer Peter Ball attended the Southend Kursaal two nights later. 'It was one of the best-ever gigs in my life,' he says. 'I'd got into SAHB about nine months previously after hearing Ding Dong and then Next. I'd only just started taking a camera to gigs and I hadn't had many decent results up til then. So I made sure we were right up at the front and I'm glad to say I took some great shots.'

A week later SAHB appeared at Hammersmith Odeon. It was the day Scotland were playing England at Wembley, and the band came on in football strips and kicked balls into the audience. The show was being recorded so the band could have one of their regular listening sessions, to make sure they still sounded as good as they could be.

During this tour Charles Shaar Murray asked Alex what rock and roll was. 'A young man's view of the future,' he replied, 'accompanied by an incredible energy. The next twenty minutes, the next twenty years – just the future.'

The Tull US tour was yet another gigantic undertaking – 22 dates over 29 days, including the 95,000–seater New Orleans Superdrome. (Alex planned to get a shark tattoo in New Orleans, but didn't find the time.) The cut-short support set was Faith Healer, Tomahawk Kid, Delilah, Gang

Peter Ball

Zal at the Southen Kursaal in 1975

Alex encouraging the audience while recording Delilah at the Hammersmith Odeon in 1975

Bang, Framed and Anthem. Delilah, a rip of the Tom Jones hit, quickly became a fans' favourite, complete as it was with Zal and Chris in another SAHB dance routine.

> **CHRIS:** Delilah was chosen purely so we could do a dance, with the aim of replacing Runaway, which had been overplayed because we gigged so much. God help us if one of us got the dance wrong, though – because the other one would kick him up the arse... Zal was an awful one for changing it – as soon as we got it right he'd get it wrong, so I thought I was getting it wrong, then we'd get it right again and he'd change it. It was just a good laugh.
>
> The Tull tour really didn't work at all – it was a profile thing. I think their music is incompatible with almost anyone else – it's not a slight, but I can't imagine who your second-favourite band is if they're your favourite...

Tull fan Danny McMillin agrees. 'I saw SAHB open for Jethro Tull in Seattle, Washington. I never heard of them before or since. They were the absolute without-a-doubt worst band I've ever had the squirming misfortune to see and hear. During the middle of the set, a kilted Alex ripped off his shirt, took a can of spray paint and wrote 'Vambo Rules!' on a fake wall. I'd have to say that was the high point of their musical abilities... After a concert of boos and yells to get off, Alex profaned the uneducated American audience in an extended colloquy, before leaving the stage after about 20 minutes of "music." I guess we just didn't get it.'

Alabama DJ Lee Moore did get it, though: 'I was at least partly prepared for the experience, being a big fan of the band on record. But nothing could have prepared me for Harvey's enormous charm. He was a master showman, a thorough professional, and his stage persona managed to be alternately intimidating and avuncular, and sometimes both at once. At one point he actually delivered a brief chiding lecture – I can't think of a more appropriate way to describe it – in the course of which he told the audience we were "very lucky boys and girls" to be living in the USA. My overall impression was that he genuinely cared about the audience on some level. He was in loco parentis, doing his part to help us shape up. The show was one of the most cleverly theatrical rock performances I've seen – Alex Harvey was right up there with Bowie – and Ian Anderson – as a consummate showman.'

Alex's 'chiding lecture' on this tour was based around the idea of America as a young nation: 'You're barely 200 years old and you have every ethnic group under the sun here,' he'd say; then, depending on how the show was going, he'd finish with, 'Don't fuck it up' or 'And you're acting like a bunch of babies'.

In the middle of the tour Mountain released the version of Delilah recorded at Hammersmith. It was probably an attempt to resolve the continuing business issue of representing the band on a single; but the recording had never been planned for release.

An eight-digit calculator with memory cost £12.95 and bargain wigs started at £2.50. Billy Connolly raised a court action against a shop calling itself 'The Big Yins' but the judge pointed out other people in Glasgow could be called 'Big Yin', recalling the phrase from a Dave Willis song. Muhammad Ali announced he'd defend his world boxing title against Jean-Pierre Coopman. And SAHB made the top ten with Delilah.

TED: We got a telegram from Bill saying, congratulations. I didn't know it was even being released. We were surprised it had been, and they did it while we were on tour. It did always go down well live…

ZAL: We got stamped with it, though – in a lot of ways it was a bad song to have a hit with. If you didn't know what the band was about it gave you a certain message. Although to be fair it actually was a fair example of what the band was about… if you knew what you were talking about.

CHRIS: Oh, aye, it stamped us alright. The next congratulatory telegram was from Les Reid and Barry Mason, who wrote Delilah, saying, well done on your hit and here's the sheet music for She's A Lady, Tom Jones' next single, if we wanted to do that…

EDDIE: But everybody loves success, and Alex had an ego the size of Glasgow… he loved glory. I don't know why it is, but when people from Glasgow make it they enjoy it all the more. I think it's because you're not expected to make it. Everyone who knew Alex, friends and family, all basked in the reflected glory.

ZAL: Financially it made no difference at all… I don't remember a big difference. There was a lot of momentum at the time. We were constantly working, touring, recording. But we were getting nearer the front page. Occasionally we'd be on the front page.

CHRIS: And they went, look, we've put it in a picture sleeve. Oh, that's great, the first 10,000 have a picture of the band on it – but what they didn't say was you lose a point of profit for a picture sleeve! And you lose a point when they do a gatefold sleeve for you – they never told you these things. And now we had a pressure we'd never had before. The record company wanted a follow-up hit straight away.

SAHB were rushed back to the UK to make an appearance on Top of the Pops. It wasn't a moment too soon – because all their gear, and the truck it was stowed in, had been stolen in Miami, two dates before the end of the Tull tour.

CHRIS: Alex's jeans were ripped up the middle, and sometimes he'd hang out of them – you could see the front row going, oooooh.... We came off after a show and everyone's body temperature is in the hundreds – and I'm like, has someone fuckin' shat themselves? And Alex goes, it might be me... and the inside of his jeans is all full of shite.

The next morning our truck was gone – the mafia stole our guitars. That's when we had to fly back for Delilah being in the charts. But we had to fly to New York first to get new guitars. So for once we were travelling first-class via Delhi to London. In those days it was £1200 a ticket. I woke up in a drunken stupour on first class, and I opened the window shutter and saw this beautiful sunrise. But the stewardess closed it again, and I'm like, twelve hundred fuckin' quid? I'll fuckin' have my sunrise... Then the senior stewardess comes up and says, sir, you can't do that – there's the Indian Ambassador sitting opposite you. I say, fuck him, he pays the same as me... So they gave me the entire upstairs bar to myself to get rid of me!

With Delilah peaking at Number 6, it was inevitable that the rest of the show was released, and the Live album came out in October. It only featured six tracks (not including the fanfare): Faith Healer, Tomahawk Kid, Vambo, Chef, Delilah and Framed – subsequent bootlegs of the whole show suggest that tinkering with the sound system rendered most other tracks unusable. All this enclosed in a sleeve which can best be described as 'shite'. Nevertheless, it had something to say for itself.

CHRIS: Sometimes on albums we gave into the temptation to do overdubs that would never be there when we were playing live, and it just cluttered things. Everyone knows you really had to see us live before the album would make sense, but concentrating on overdubs didn't make that any easier for people. That's why Live really worked.

But the thing was, the American label refused to release it, saying live albums didn't sell. Next year Peter Frampton came alive and that was it. But they'd never take a risk, that was the thing. We weren't big enough to do our own headline tour in the States and we couldn't get our message across... Live would have helped – and I'm saying that even though we never wanted it released.

Having said all that, I only realised how big we'd been in America when I played there with other bands. The thing is, we didn't get the chance to play with other people, jam with them or anything. That only came later, like when I was with Michael Schenker and I was in the biggest band in the world: me, Angus Young, Malcolm Young, Robin Zander and Rick Neilsen – but we were all playing the wrong instruments! But playing with the guys from Cheap Trick, I found out how big SAHB fans they were. When Schenker supported Cheap Trick there was this banner hanging off the balcony: Cheap Trick You Suck, Bring Back SAHB! Robin and Rick were fine with it, but I was like, what the fuck's going on?

The testament of fan Jon Macleod proves Live would have worked in the States. 'It was fall 1975, and I had just become a raving Kiss fanatic – I've since learned better, but hey, I wasn't alone back then! Some rock mag ran an article on freak bands, leading with Kiss, so I had to have a look; and they included SAHB, a name I filed away for future reference. Shortly after that, I tripped over Live in the record store. The cover immediately grabbed my attention – believe it or not – and I scanned it closely. These were those guys, huh? I still remember the thing that hit me hardest was the spreadeagle photo of Zal on the back. I thought, these guys have got to be cool.

'So I got it home. Fanfare came on... uh-oh: horns! For a moment I was afraid this was a big mistake – I wanted *rock*. Horns don't rock. But then, of course, Faith Healer started up – and there was my rock. God, the impact of that song for the first time still resonates after fuckin' decades! The spooky throbbing intro – never heard anything like it – that opening riff, Alex's incantation, more spook, Ted's double drum roll... and then Zal hit that two-string-chord riff for the first time. And I knew true awe!

'I hung amazed on every note for the rest of the song. Hugh was the first rock keyboardist I'd heard who was actually an asset to the band. Alex's performance was chilling. I was in the presence of an instant classic and I knew it! The rest of the album grabbed damn near as hard, and I got a feel for the unique story-music world of SAHB. This band was powerful, accomplished, inimitable, entertaining and inspiring in a way no rock band was before or since. Chef was strange and epic, Delilah and Framed were hilarious. I played the album nonstop for days afterward. I lucked out big-time finding it.'

By this time SAHB were back in the US of A again, on a tour that included two dates with Tear Gas idol Frank Zappa – an idol Zal was too scared to meet.

CHRIS: Alex and I spent half an hour in his dressing room. He was great. He talked about the most mundane things and the most interesting things. He was tuning his guitar the whole time but he was saying, I don't know why I'm bothering, I got the best neck, the best strings, it's half an hour from here to the stage and the temperature's different – so I hit the first chord and the fuckin' thing's out! I remember he wanted to hire our pipers. It might have been the only reason he was talking to us... But he didn't realise we only used them for Anthem, that it wasn't easy to make them part of a tune, and they didn't just jam along. I think he was quite disappointed.

TED: I wasn't ready for the strength of some of the stuff we smoked in America. We were in New Orleans with Zappa. When I turned up there was a wee guy playing my drumkit – he must have

Mandy Hathway

been about 8 or 9 – grooving away and it sounded great. At the time I just went, wow that's fantastic... but after the show photographer Chuck Pulin gave me something to smoke and my paranoia kicked in. I thought, are they going to replace me with this wee guy, just for sheer sensationalism? At the time I thought SAHB could do anything, and WOULD do anything to get attention, so this made perfect sense to me.

Then I realised they'd need to get rid of me first, and I became convinced they were going to have me shot! So Dick O'Dell said it was time to go, and I followed him out and realised it was just him and me in the car park... And I just knew: Dick was going to shoot me so they could get the wee drummer boy in. It made so much sense to me I agreed with the sentiment – the album sales would go through the roof!

I believed I was gettin' it right up to the moment Dick opened the boot – and no shotgun! So we went back to the hotel and there was a guy in a big

Dick O'Dell

raincoat in the foyer and I thought, aaaah, HE'S gonny shoot me! By this time I was feeling so hyper I wanted to be shot! Birdfeather was a Sicilian who might well have mafia connections, and again it all made perfect sense...

Well, after a while I felt better and told Birdfeather and Chuck what I thought was going on – and of course they just dismissed it. We headed out to a club and I sat on my own, and again I became

Ian Dickson

Hugh, Chris, Alex, Ted and Zal take a bow after one of London's Christmas shows

convinced they were going to shoot me. I think Birdfeather was feeling sorry for me because everyone was having a good time and I wasn't, so she came over and did the worst thing she could possibly do. She kissed me. *The mafia kiss of death!* So this is it – they're not gonny shoot me, they're gonny haul me across the pool table and stab me through the heart!

I can only call the whole episode a momentary lapse of Coatbridge.

It may have been a relief – certainly for some blood-sweating band members – to head home again, but there was one more trick to be pulled out of the hat in 1975: the Christmas gigs. These seven sell-out shows – four in the New Victoria in London around Christmas and three in the Apollo in Glasgow around Hogmanay – are legendary to this day, and were the crowning glory of the band's live performance. The published intent was to thank the fans for what had arguably been a stunningly successful year – and in the event the band lost £100 over the series of gigs.

The Bay City Rollers were at the top of the US charts with Saturday Night and the top twenty albums of the year included Tubular Bells, Dark Side of the Moon and Atlantic Crossing. The Sex Discrimination Act became law while Chrysler bosses told the unions if they didn't accept 8500 job losses the company would go under. Scots queued for over five hours to see Jaws, Bing Crosby appeared in a TV add for Tennents Lager and European secret services were ordered to assassinate Carlos the Jackal. And meanwhile, SAHB's Christmas concerts were truly, genuinely, unforgettable and irreplaceably sensational.

ZAL: That was the pinnacle. Everything focussed on that. We spent loads of time rehearsing, we had the dancers, we had this phenomenal stage set. Nothing was ever better than that. It was meticulous, like rehearsing a west end show. That was the culmination of our choreography – you be on that mark at 45 minutes in and pull this face, you be up the ladder on the hour, that light's going to come on then so be there for it... And it all went like clockwork.

TED: The Apollo had the warmest, most emotional audience you could get. And we had the show just right, the talent contest and everything. People had a whole night's entertainment – there was never a pause. And it was all three balconies then, with the top one going doing–doing–doing... The message was strong. Alex was very strong. The saddest thing is it was never filmed.

ZAL: He was in his element. You could see him strutting around the place, conducting, directing, kissing the dancers' arses, performing at his peak, on top of it.

EDDIE: There's a lot of dominant characters in that band. Zal become one – even though he's seen as a quiet man he could be quite vociferous at times. I never saw them that good ever...

The main element of the stage set was a Christmas present, which opened and folded down to reveal the band. The show featured bare-bum dancers who flashed their assets during Dancing Cheek To Cheek (two of them later appeared in the UK sitcom Hi-De-Hi), an ambitious live rendition of Stone Eater, and a hilarious piece of theatre known as the talent show.

CHRIS: It started off with Zal tap dancing on a metal tray, reciting the soliloquay from Hamlet. Then big Robbie, the six-foot giant with the PA company, would come on with a leotard and a crash helmet on. Alex would say, this is an illegitimate son of Lord Longford, who was expelled from Eton for palming a jockstrap during a game of strip poker... And Robbie would do the hula hoop. I had to come on as Glen Benson, with a big cowboy hat and boots up to my knees, and sing Laughing The Blues. Then Hugh would come on with the accordion and give it the folk music treatment. It was always rigged so Hugh won it...

Ian Dickson

The Christmas gigs lineup: Chris, Hugh, Alex, Zal and Hugh with bare-arsed singers

We had boxes for our parents in the Apollo. Ted gave his parents earplugs, the pink wax ones you got from Boots. During the second song Ted's dad leaned over to his mum and said, they sweeties were horrible!

I sent a limousine for my mum and dad but my dad told the guy to go away because he hadn't called a taxi! So I sent the same driver the next night, and during the show we let him stay in the dressing room. He was sitting in a big huge bubble chair with its back to the room so you didn't know he was there. The three dancers came off to change and just as they're all stark naked he rotated the chair round to be confronted with three six–foot blondes. They weren't bothered at all – they were like, how're you getting on, pal? So he wouldn't take any money from me at the end of the night. He was like, I'll dine out on this for ever...

Zal's guitar fucked up during Dance to the Music and after the show I came into the dressing room and Zal's face was tripping him. I said, okay, the guitar broke down – no big deal. He said, it's nothing to do with the guitar breaking down. It was the first time I heard you all playing and you're going like a train! And here's me thinking it was all down to me! I'm overplaying! And when I wasn't playing it didn't make a difference!

And during Framed Alex asked the crowd, do you believe me? And someone shouted back, Naw – you shagged my sister in 1971! The Apollo... what a place. Dougie was getting the guitars set up, coming back and forward from the tuning room, so he's on his way back and he sees this bloke coming down with one of our guitars. Who the fuck are you? he asks, and the guy answers, Oh, I'm taking this guitar down for Dougie... He goes, I'm fuckin' Dougie... Smack! But they gave us an award for being the first band to sell out the Apollo three nights in a row.

Paisley boy Jack McDougall is one of many SAHBsters who remembers that Christmas fondly. 'My neighbour, Charlie, knew Alex very well, and one night I sat and listened to his stories when they came back from the pub. He had hundreds – he'd go off in a tangent telling other tales, but he always came back to his original story, a–la Billy Connolly. I took them all in, although whether I believed them or not is another story... I never asked him if he'd really been a lion–tamer but I did ask him to tell me the story of Isobel Goudie. After a lesson on the history of witchcraft he said he'd tell me where to find the spot where the last witch was burned at the stake in Scotland. He said he'd tell me at the Apollo.

'So at one of those three shows he sat down at the edge of the stage and told a witchy story. It was a three–thousand sell out, but I felt the story was only for me. Then he explained where to find the spot. Next day, I headed to the crossroads beside the Maxwellton Bar, waited for a break in the traffic, ran into the middle of the road – and there it was: a horseshoe embedded in the concrete. Alex's story had been true. Again. I still look at the horseshoe every time I pass.'

CONSENTING TOMATOES Z

ZAL ON TOMORROW BELONGS TO ME

The echo of the last album had only just subsided. It had even captivated the Americans with a mixture of dislocated humour and moments of sensational parody. Only, just as your heart begins to reconcile these things, back in the garage in North London we sat as if the eternal stream had blown dry and mutated. There seemed to be no escape; we were to be part of something forever unsettled – but the arid processes of doubt and speculation were finally blown away.

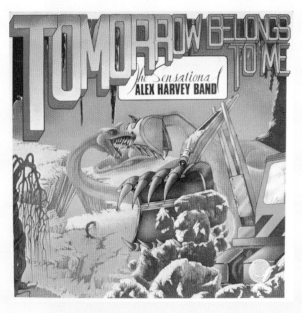

Tomorrow is an album that continues to enforce SAHB's energy for self-mutilating diversity. And as with all SAHB albums there was one track that presupposes an immediate way out. It was the one great chocolate in the box; and this time the song was Chef.

Action Strasse: Chug-chug meets dusky maiden rummaging around in your trousers. What a circus routine that would make!

Snake Bite: Recorded in the famous Apple Studios. Feedback guitar solo shows what a great producer Dave is...

Soul in Chains: Extreme innuendo about consenting tomatoes – I think!

The Tale of the Giant Stone Eater: Conservation for the 21st century; a delightful opus whose alliteration is bound up in biospheres and the brutality of progress.

Ribs & Balls: Funky bastard of a riff. Alex loved this kind of shit and fails to keep a straight face throughout. See? I told you this band has no shame.

Give My Compliments to the Chef: Something of a masterpiece – and again it's Alex's lyrical mischievousness and Hugh's striking mood that sets up the groove.

Sharks Teeth: Jazz confusion of dubious parentage. Love the Richard Widmark line and the south sea strum in the middle. Indulgent, in-house humour that rarely transmits...

Shake That Thing: How *dare* they record a track without me?

Tomorrow Belongs to Me: Now Cabaret was a great movie, but what the fuck is this all about? Crassness that still rebounds like a monkey fuckin' a weasel.

To Be Continued: Bear with me on this one!

Ray Conn

Before a show in 1976: this page, Chris and Ted (top), Zal and Hugh (below); right, Alex limbering up

5 SAHB STORIES

EVERYONE thought the band had arrived. The bean counters who cared about pounds and pence saw a product drawing between two and three million a year. The fashion victims who needed social approval before liking anything saw a pop group which had achieved a top-ten hit and top-twenty albums. The fans, the real people, the folk who mattered... they knew the band had arrived years ago. Because it was never about pounds and pence or tens and twenties – it was about top top quality entertainment with honesty, conviction, understanding and love.

CHRIS: We were mobbed after the Christmas gigs – that was us stars. We were so big, I couldn't walk down the street without being accosted. It sounds funny but it's terrible – you can't go for a burger or anything. Everyone who has the slightest connection with you wants a piece of you, and that's fine – *if* they pick their moment. But too many people want you at the same time and you're just swamped. My dad and my six-year-old son were at the Apollo gig and when they went to the toilet my boy told someone, my dad's Chris Glen, and this my grandad... So my dad comes out and says, tell that boy not to tell people who I am. I had to sign autographs while I'm having a pish!

When I did the Apollo with Schenker I took Cozy Powell to a wee pub nearby, and he was saying it must have been great going there when I was in SAHB. But the truth was there's no way I could have gone in there at that time. It sounds like I'm whining but I'm not – it's out of respect for fans that we avoided them. There's no way we could give them the time they deserved, and it's better for it not to happen at all than for someone to think, what a twat, he's too big to gig, not stopping to talk for long...

HUGH: I never considered myself famous in any way. Alex was the star. Zal was his foil – he performed more than anyone else, but of course he wasn't known facially at all. Chris stood up and pulled poses as well, then myself and Ted were sitting down. I did get stopped in the street and asked for autographs – I'd maybe walk from Glasgow Central to Buchanan Street, and maybe three or four people would stop me. But I didn't consider myself a famous person – I considered myself part of a successful band.

ZAL: The idea of being a guitar hero was always slightly tongue-in-cheek for me. You're always trying to get better, listening to Jeff Beck or John McLaughlin or Frank Zappa and going, how do I play that? It's part of the soul music upbringing. When something moves me musically and spiritually, my adrenaline goes sky-high and I want to get up and do something about it – that's when I go to the front of the stage and start presenting it. I'm saying, this feels good to me... do you want to have some of this? You should be sharing this feeling! And they do – that's what you get back. It's adulation but it's not really for me. It's not, look at me, I'm a star – it's a shared experience. And when that works, when you get it back... yeah, this is fun... So it's not about fame at all.

Runaway-style: Hugh, Chris, Alex, Zal and Ted

Alex may or may not have wanted to be rich and famous; but as frontman of the hottest band in the country the only way past the mountain was to keep climbing. In a touching aside, Ted tells how Alex heard his son Alex jnr was having a few problems with local youths, and went up north to sort it out. Alex still had time for people – even if he was pressed.

Mountain had decided to end SAHB's relationship with Phonogram in favour of a distribution deal with EMI; so the band were required to close the deal with one more album. They took the opportunity to underline the humourous element of their attitude and record a set of covers. The result was the Penthouse Tapes, with its accompanying single, Runaway – even though they'd long since stopped playing the track.

TED: idea was, let's stick on all the covers, this is a good place to do that. But we thought, let's fart about and try to do impressions of people. For example, I Wanna Have You Back was us doing an impression of Gary Glitter. And Love Story was a great trick – we'd done it in Tear Gas but we kept it in SAHB. You started really quiet and then threw the crowd against the back wall...

DAVE: The arrangement for Love Story came about because Tear Gas were playing some miner's social somewhere, and we'd been told to keep quiet – keep it doon' lads – so we thought we were doing that. But the guy came up to us after the first set and said, ye'll no' get yer pie an' beans if ye don't tone it right down... By this time we were really pissed off, so we went on and did Love Story, with Zal picking the riff on his own, really tentative and empty, and then we threw it out on the second verse... and that's how it came about.

Peter Ball

Alex eating a rose at the Southend Kursaal in 1976. Some fans still have the petals he threw into the audience.

A WORD ABOUT THESE OLD TAPES WE FOUND ONE MORNING WHILE CLEANING THE PENTHOUSE— WE'VE DONE THEM ALL ON STAGE AND KEEP BEING REQUESTED — ANYWAY YOU CAN'T HAVE NEW SONGS WITHOUT OLD SONGS — RIGHT!

I WANNA HAVE YOU BACK

A POP SONG WRITTEN SUDDENLY IN SILENT FURY— INSPIRED BY SOME RIFF ZAL RIPPED OFF.

JUNGLE JENNY

GORILLA—THE LARGEST & STRONGEST OF THE PRIMATES (MAN-LIKE APES) FIRST REPORTED BY HANNO THE CARTHAGIAN 450 B.C. — LATER DU CHAILLU VISITED ITS HABITAT EARLY 19th CENTURY— NEEDLESS TO SAY NOBODY BELIEVED ANY OF THEM UNTIL CAPTAIN HARRIS DELIVERED A SKELETON TO THE BRITISH MUSEUM IN 1851 — AS FAR AS IS KNOWN JUNGLE JENNY IS STILL WORKING AS A LIPSTICK TESTER FOR WILLY AND HIS WALNUTS —OK!

RUNAWAY

WE WISH WE COULD WRITE SONGS LIKE THIS.

LOVE STORY

WRITTEN BY AND DEDICATED TO IAN ANDERSON & HIS GROOVY TULL GUYS WHO HELPED US WHEN WE WERE IN NEED;

SCHOOLS OUT

REMEMBER THE ZEBRA CROSSING.

IRENE GOODNIGHT

WRITTEN BY THE IMMORTAL HUDDY LEADBETTER — WROTE IT HE DID IN JAIL FOR THE GOVERNORS DAUGHTER— GAVE HIM AN IMMEDIATE PARDON— DON'T BELIEVE ME ASK YOUR HISTORY TEACHER — IF HE DON'T KNOW FIND ANOTHER SCHOOL.

IF YOU ONLY SAY YOU'RE MINE

I WROTE THIS SONG 23 YEARS AGO AND IT'S FOR GEORDIE K — DARKY— THE LAZY Y— LOS APACHES — THE STAG — UNCLE JIMMY — BANJO CHUCK — DICK — SID — CHARLIE — RAB— GRIMES— CAMPBELL AND EVERYBODY WHO EVER SHARED THEIR BEANS WITH THE DUNOON PIER DWELLERS.

CRAZY HORSES

WHY NOT? FIRST TIME WE DID THIS WAS BUXTON FESTIVAL — FIRST NUMBER— STOPPED THE RAIN.

GAMBLING BAR ROOM BLUES

WRITTEN & RECORDED BY THE DADDY OF ALL COUNTRY AND WESTERN MUSIC — JIMMY RODGERS THE SINGING BRAKE-MAN — DURING AMERICAS DEPRESSION — IT'S STILL A GREAT SONG FROM A GREAT COUNTRY.

CHEEK TO CHEEK

"HAVEN'T I HEARD THAT SONG BEFORE", SAID GEORGE FINEGLOVE TO SARAH SPINETHRUST WHILE SAHB WERE RECORDING LIVE IN THE NEW VICTORIA THEATRE IN LONDON XMAS 1975.

"YES", SAID SARAH, "FRED ASTAIRE DOES IT — BUT HE REALLY DOES IT WELL".

WELL THAT'S ABOUT IT FOLKS WE HOPE YOU ENJOY THE SONGS.

SEE YOU SOON,

Alex

Above, Alex's sleeve notes which accompanied the Penthouse Tapes release; below, the front and back images on the album cover show a 'before and after' sequence

Ian Dickson

A publicity shot from a 1976 series the label said were 'too weird' to use

Promo poster for the Who stadium tour

Brian Hogg regards the album highly. 'I loved the fact there was so much humour. Let's do the Osmonds – what a great attitude! So funny, and yet done with so much love. I think, along with Next, the Penthouse Tapes sum up the whole ethos of the band.'

Reviewer Geoff Barton said: 'No group but SAHB could have recorded this album and carried it off successfully. If a young, up-and-coming outfit, anxious to secure a record contract, had hawked around various companies with tapes on a par to this LP, they would have become a laughing stock. If an older, established band, noted for their serious approach, had suddenly come up with a platter similar to this one, they'd be dismissed as having turned demented. For SAHB, it works. The Penthouse Tapes is more alcohol-besotten than Gamblin' Bar Room Blues, is the campness of Delilah multiplied a dozen times, is crazier than Action Strasse and Snake Bite combined. Deranged, neurotic, scatty... and it's also very good. Tongue-in-cheek, spontaneous and good-time.'

Unsurprisingly the band were soon touring again, with another trip round the island; but the pressure was beginning to tell and nerves were beginning to fray. Nevertheless, the first few dates went well, with critics welcoming new material that was to appear on the band's next 'real' album.

Fan and photographer Peter Ball was back at the Southern Kursaal. 'I was really looking forward to this one, but I wasn't ready for the big metal barrier about three feet from the stage,' he recalls. 'It's the only time I ever saw this setup at the Kursaal. It was exactly level with my stomach. Alex came on wearing a bearskin hat holding a rose, which he proceeded to eat – and the audience went nuts! Everybody surged forward, crushing me against the barrier. I managed to get a few photos but the pressure from the crowd took its toll and I ended up fainting and being dragged out by the security men, barely hanging onto the camera. I came to almost immediately and they ushered me over the barrier at one side of the stage, so I had to put up with people's heads and amp stacks blocking my view for the rest of the show. They were on top form though – they finished with an incredibly powerful version of Framed.'

From Newcastle, Angie Errigo reported: 'It's in the meaty new numbers, Dance to Your Daddy and Amos Moses, that the band is most impressive, with locomotive riffs and Hugh McKenna's power-driving on keyboards characterising the former, harmonic precision and Ted McKenna's muscular drumming highlighting the latter. The current SAHB Theatre Presentation features Zal in dejected mime attempting to wrestle, cajole and bribe his guitar away from the wily Alex, popping up like Punch out of the upper window of the tenement backdrop. The kids provide 'aaah's and 'yay's like kids at a pantomime and cheer Zal's success through an unlikely, classically-styled solo on amplified acoustic guitar.

'Then Alex appears overhead with new lyrics, written that day, clutched in his hand for the best parody of Hitler since Chaplin's The Great Dictator. Wearing a milk carton swastika and a string of sellotape moustaches on his sleeve which he peels off and slaps on one after the other as they slop off his lip, he complains, "I vas freymed".

'The Glen, Harvey and Cleminson trio goose-step to the front of the stage, Alex griping about being bombed in his bunker and bombed in his balls and succeeding completely in stitching up the chicification of fascism. It's a continuous thorn in Harvey's side that the band's comicstrip pastiches of violence and nastiness have been taken as read and criticised. "Now you listen," he splutters after Framed, "That was good fun, but don't you think for one minute that we think that bastard was a good man."'

TWO weeks later, the rock star lifestyle caved in on Hugh, and he suffered a severe breakdown. The official line at the time came from a Mountain spokesman: 'At first it was thought he was suffering from a virus but doctors said he was completely exhausted as the result of overwork, and he has been ordered to rest for at least two weeks.' The truth, sadly, was more unsettling.

ZAL: It was at the Colston Hall, Bristol. Hugh just stopped playing and decided to jump off the front stage and get a light. Then he sat down in the front row just watching the band. Someone later told me he'd forgotten he was in the band...

TED: It was all very painful for me – he's my cousin, I've known him since I was young and he'd been a musical collaborator for years... I'd had to take him to this horrible old hospital. He was putting his clothes back on after the doctor checked him over, saying, right, let's go Ted. I had to tell him, no, Hugh, you've got to stay here. And they gave him one of those horrible green backless gowns and I had to leave him in this Victorian gothic sanitarium-like place.

Hugh never wanted to play it Alex's way. His sense of music wouldn't let him twist it the way Alex wanted to do it. So he always had to work against that, and he'd often become the rebel.

But Alex said, if we all believe in Hugh we can will him out of his bad state of mind. And I wanted to believe him, I wanted it to be true. I couldn't bear the thought of Hugh having to stay in hospital, and not being in the band. But it was Chris who said, look, can we live with ourselves if we try to make him keep going in the band and he gets worse?

CHRIS: No one wanted him back more than me, but I was making the point, is it right for Hugh to come back? It was never that it might be a hassle, but was it a hassle for Hugh? Especially given that the lifestyle was partly responsible.

We visited him in hospital and asked if we could get him anything, and he said he'd like a watch. So next time we brought him a watch, he put it on and said, it's 8.20... now it's 8.21... now it's 8.22... Why did we get him the fuckin' watch?

ZAL: The problem was, the band was so busy and caught up in being SAHB, there's wasn't enough time to sit and think – there was no qualification about how ill he was. We just thought it was an episode and it would be over soon. He was ill but SAHB still had to go to Europe.

CHRIS: One of the doctors said his perfect job would be greenkeeper on a bowling green, playing piano at the weekend.

TED: To which I would say, what the fuck did he know? There's no doubting Hugh's massive talent and it would have been a shame to waste it. But the lifestyle didn't suit him. He seemed to enjoy it but he was too intense – less intense than Chris maybe, but with Chris it was a career choice...

Incredibly the band only missed one date of the tour. Tommy Eyre filled Hugh's shoes for the remaining dates, fresh from a stint with Nazareth on their UK tour. Tommy had made his name with the stunning arrangement of Joe Cocker's By With A Little Help – Lennon once said it was the best arrangement of a Beatles song he'd ever heard. So, well worth the £50 Tommy was paid for arranging and playing on it...

By the end of the tour Hugh felt ready to return, just in time for a last-minute addition to the band's schedule: a stadium tour with the Who, Little Feat and the Outlaws. Despite the fact SAHB had only just finished their own tour, their addition to the three-date event kicked up ticket sales significantly. They were paid more than the Who for their appearance at Charlton Athletic, Celtic and Swansea football grounds. In case of emergencies, Tommy Eyre was at the gigs too.

CHRIS: Harvey Goldsmith, the promoter, wasn't sure it was going to sell out. So he looked for someone who would secure that, but we were an albatross because everyone had just seen us. So it was a risk, but Harvey wanted to take it. Until we were announced Charlton had sold 17,000 tickets, after we were announced it sold 51,000. I'm not saying we sold 34,000 tickets, but the idea of the Who plus Little Feat plus us made 34,000 people decide, aye alright, we'll go.

Charlton was over the odds – the capacity was something like 26,000 and Harvey got 51,000 in there. And it was raining. So there was a bit of violence – but no wonder. I mean, in an average town of 50,000 people how much trouble will there be in a day? It didn't pertain to us or the Who or Little Feat or anything. But if Alex saw something going down we'd stop playing, and he would either stop the fight or ask security to deal with it. Then Ted would go one, two, three, four and we'd pick it up again.

I felt quite bad for Little Feat. We loved them, but it was a laid-back American vibe you smoked a joint to and that doesn't work when it's pissing with rain. When it's battering off your heid what do you want to do, kick back or shout 'my my my Delilah'? Charlton was tailor-made for us because they needed what we were giving them.

Then the night before we played at Celtic Park, it's me and Keith Moon and all the guys from the

A ticket from the legendary Who gig at Parkhead in 1976

Who, coked out our skulls, pissed out our brains. Keith had stolen Harvey's megaphone, and he opened the window and announced, 'This is not a drill, this is a bomb scare, evacuate the building!' So we think it's hilarious, and half an hour later six policemen turn up... We're under arrest for breach of the peace. So we're being taken down this big long corridor, I'm last in the line, and a door opens and it's Ted's wife Tracy. Quick as a flash I'm in through the door... what an escape!

Harvey was mad for his salads. He said, it's summer, people want salads. I told him, nah, this is Glasgow, sell Scotch pies and Bovril... So he set up 30,000 salads and in the end he was left with 26,000! A few years back I asked him what happened to them... He said, dunno, we left them in Celtic's bootroom... Can you imagine opening that room the week the season started?

But we insisted on having Celtic's dressing room – Zal went along with it – and I hung my clothes on Jimmy Johnstone's number 7 hook.

In an interesting quirk of north-south division, the Scottish press suggested that SAHB were better than the Who at Parkhead, while the English press either carefully avoided the issue or stuck to the belief the headline act were the winners. There's no doubt the Who had a run for their money, though. Before they went on Alex advised them: 'Don't be shite – there are 400 cousins of mine in the audience...' During his own set Alex had congratulated the audience for being so well-behaved. Even the usual Celtic-Rangers rivalry had been dampened down for the day; except for right at the beginning of the show, when a wisp of smoke floated across the stage area, and some bluenose yelled: 'That's it, Alex – burn the fuckin' place doon!'

CHRIS: The Who were much bigger than us, they were legendary, they'd done Woodstock... so when some press said, '...and the Who blew SAHB off stage', who the fuck were we that it needed saying? So I think that answers the question. Everyone expected to see the Who being the Who, they maybe weren't expecting to get another band being so good... They got £10,000 a gig for three gigs, we got £15,000 for Charlton, £12,000 for Swansea and £12,000 for Parkhead.

The Charlton story stuck, though. Melody Maker published an article by Allan Jones on violence at festivals, which suggested SAHB promoted antisocial behaviour during their shows. The next week, Harvey Goldsmith wrote in to defend the band: 'We have just completed a 31-date tour with SAHB and have had no trouble or damage at any of the halls, except for the normal ambient problems of the public leaving their seats for the encores. Many times I have seen Alex Harvey speak to an audience who appeared to be getting over-exuberant, and ask them to go back to their seats, and I certainly remember Alex praising the audience for being such a good audience and not causing any problems.'

Allan, always a staunch fan, had discussed the theme of violence with SAHB before. 'One senses that the implications are all too real in the context of Alex's vision,' he wrote once. 'They tread a dangerous line between militant anarchy and utopian pacifism, underlined with a kind of relentless humour that somehow balances the inherent paradox of their situation. The Framed routine is relentlessly violent, then Alex will introduce Anthem as a hymn for peace. It veers from being a threat to being a call for peace, and as a climax is unbeatable.'

Meanwhile Alex had told Charles Shaar Murray: 'It's better if a tough punk act is just a fantasy, because the real thing is so horrible. I've seen two people shot dead in front of me, and if it's not a fantasy, then you're gonna die of a broken heart. You're gonna say, look at those poor people, look at what they've done to each other. It's much better for it all just to be a fantasy. Or a comic book...'

Later in the year Alex would speak of the situation again. 'I don't like to spout on too much about this. I don't want to become political. You know that Melody Maker attack about us being violent? I thought up a million ways of attacking that back. I was going to take two pages and quote the Yes concert when we stopped a fight for them. Sometimes I think the wrong impression gets taken because of the kind of kids we get. A lot of them are street kids. But I think they're the salt of the earth and if their direction, their energy can be channelled in some direction that's for the good of the community rather than destroying themselves, then that's a good thing.'

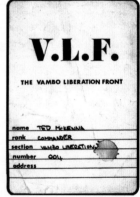

Ted's VLF card

ZAL: I didn't really think Alex was aware of everything he was doing and the effect it had, but the way he puts it there, it's the opposite – he *did* have a crusade about wayward kids and all that. The Glasgow thing again – there's a better life out there than running round slashing people. Fuck, he was such a hippy...

Some people may not have got it, but Alex's point was getting through to plenty of folk: the Vambo Liberation Front, for example. Inspired by the 'never vandal be' character, around 200 squatters and street kids got together in Sussex and created their own organisation, aiming to 'minimise what the modern city can do to us'. These rough types engaged in a series of social programmes, including helping local dossers to reconnect with society. Alex met their committee and was impressed: 'I don't give a shit about putting on a good show – the important thing is these boys and girls, those babies.'

SOMEWHERE in time SAHB managed to record yet another album: SAHB Stories, which Charles Shaar Murray hailed as 'a surprisingly mature performance and a tremendously encouraging demonstration of the band's genuine growth. This is the first album they've made which functions perfectly and succeeds totally as a record, and doesn't require a viewing of the latest incarnation of the stage show to render it complete.' This may be in part due to Alex's new policy of letting the band have their way in a lot more directions; a move, he told the press, which satisfied with because it made him less of a leader and more of an example-setter. SAHB Stories features the only non-Harvey SAHB compositions the band recorded: Dogs of War, written completely by Zal, and Sirocco, a Hugh-only creation.

CHRIS: We wrote it all in my garage – I'd bought a house and wanted something for me, so I set the garage up as a studio. Me, my wife, Zal and the roadies refitted it – when we glued the cork boards to the ceiling we all ended up high as kites on the fumes. It was just a wee room, but there was a bonsai drumkit with an 18-inch bass, a few wee amps and a small PA. That's where we wrote the rest of our albums.

ZAL: It was an attempt to be as commercial as we could possibly be, responding to those pressures from management. For a lot of people it has good continuity, the songs work...

HUGH: We'd all been sitting in Chris' lounge and Alex asked me to come out to the garage for half an hour. He showed me the lyrics for Boston Tea Party, set up this drum groove and said, 'I'm going to switch the tape recorder on, just play and sing what you like.' I just sang the whole thing through in one go and that was it. The only other time that happened was Stone Eater.

CHRIS: It's a great groove – it's an easy song to listen to. But the tempo is so important. When we do it live you'll hear me screaming at Ted, it's too fuckin' fast, slow it right down... it's got a lovely swing and if you don't keep it that way there's no point doing it. If you let it start too fast it's a Status Quo song by the end!

TED: $25 For A Massage was based on an experience one of us had in America... We were jamming the riff in the studio and Alex came in and just started putting lyrics over the top. He often did that – he'd suddenly give the song a name then work out lyrics to fit the name he'd given it. $25 was a one-take song.

ZAL: Jungle Rub Out was another one of those things. Not what I'd call real songs – they were throwaways, B-sides – we never did any of them live. Good to play, good fun, but they wouldn't do the business for a live show.

The album also featured Dance To Your Daddy, which Alex claimed was a part of the Vibrania Suite: 'Something we've concepted,' he explained, 'that might end up as a West End show or something.' This mythical piece was to haunt the band for the rest of their days – even into the twenty-first century, with Zal's novel, Hail Vibrania, based on the concept, being published chapter by chapter on the band's website. The premise is this: Vibrania is a country, Vambo its ambassador. It's a very gentle nation and they've done away with all rules, except for one vicious law: citizens can commit two crimes, from littering to murder, and go free; but when you commit your third crime you die instantly. The concept has generated a lot of interest over the years.

Jack McDougall had his copy of SAHB Stories stolen – by Alex. 'On the day it was released, Alex visited my neighbour Charlie. Over I went to get my albums signed, including the brand new one. He hadn't heard the finished article before – and he wasn't happy! It was something to do with record companies and the way they recycle the vinyl cuttings to get more albums out, but I didn't follow it. Anyway, he asked if he could take my copy back to London the next day. As a starstruck sixteen–year–old I said yes, but I was totally gutted. Two weeks later a box arrived for me, and inside were both Tear Gas albums, loads of photos, and a new "factory sample" SAHB Stories. I was sure Alex would have forgotten all about taking it, but he didn't.'

1976 tour programme: The attempt at turning Alex's comic-book theme into a programme perhaps lacked the quality of SAHB's live shows, while launching the band's alter-egos as Teacher (Alex), Actor (Zal), Punk (Chris), Professor (Hugh) and Buffer (Ted)

SAHB Stories also gave the band their biggest hit, after they won a battle with Mountain to have Boston Tea Party released. It made the top ten in July 1976, when Elton John had his first number one (Don't Go Breaking My Heart with Kiki Dee), sharing the charts with The Boys Are Back In Town, Let's Stick Together and Leader of the Pack. A Skoda S100 was £1079, an Alba music centre was £128 and the British music industry was worth £500,000,000 a year in exports. The Queen appealed to the president of Angola to spare four white mercenaries sentenced to death; John Lennon won his battle to stay in the USA; the Olympics were on red alert as a suicide squad headed for Montreal, and one of those saltires in the sky appeared over Scotland, to be taken as an omen for independence.

It charted slightly lower than Delilah but stayed in the game longer – maybe suggesting the band had a better grip on commercial reality than the label. The exercise in exchanging views had led the band members to start asking questions; and the more they asked, the more they doubted.

CHRIS: Everyone said, we want to do Tea Party as a single. But the management didn't want to do it, the record company didn't want to do it – and you start worrying, will they promote it if we force it through? You knew they'd promote a single *they* wanted, but would they promote Tea Party?

We were going to do Top of the Pops and this big limo came to get me and Zal, hung around all day and then took us home again. We were thinking, this is all very well but who's paying for it? We found out it cost £150 so we went to Mountain and said, give us £50 each and we'll make our own way in next time... They said, you can't because it's all tax–deductable and all that...

Another thing about Top of the Pops was, you'd go to the BBC bar afterwards and there'd be all these A&R guys patting themselves on the back saying, well we did it, we got them in the top twenty. Or if something didn't chart they'd be saying, what can you do if the material's not there? It never had anything to do with the band to these people – it was all down to them. The fact we'd spent years building up our own following meant nothing.

ON 28 July 1976, Bill Fehilly, his son, two business partners and the pilot were killed when their plane crashed. Bill had been the band's mentor and biggest fan, and was renowned as the only man

who could control Alex. His personal influence had been unending, and it was apparent to everyone things would never be the same again – both in business and real life.

Pictures of Alex at the funeral show a man on the edge; the steeled resolve that held him through Les' death was gone. Alex would later write about his feelings in No Complaints Department. In a very real sense it was the beginning of the end.

EDDIE: Alex only trusted Bill. He never trusted anyone else. He had good cause to mistrust; let's be honest, if you hadn't been ripped off you weren't in the rock business. It was standard that the band got nothing while the management carved it up. When Les died, he felt the family should have got money, that the band or crew were at fault and there should have been some compensation. Alex said he'd spoken to Bill about it and Bill was

Alex at Bill's funeral

going to pursue it – Bill never told me that, but Alex did – and when Bill died all that was lost. I think he felt so alone after that, and he spoke of it.

CHRIS: He genuinely was the seventh son of a seventh son. He was a SAHB fanatic. He really cared

JULY 28, 1976

FOR BILL - They TOLD US you Were DEAD
IT brought Bitter News to Hear, Tears of sadness to shed
A MAN SO dynAMic and so strong
So MUch of A BiG DADDy to US ALL
ALL who CAME TO KNOW HiM
FROM the MildEST TO the highesT
COULD feel the powerful FORCE
which BILL radiated in abundance
HE EffecteD all OUR LiVES
SOMETIMES through his KINDNESS
OTHER TIMES through his MIGHT
BUT the seUenth SON of a seventh SON
IS A LEGEND iN HIS OWN TIME
AND COMMands his due respect and dignity
This BiG MAN WAs proUD
AND PAINTED HIS MArK iN BOLD STROKES
He had an instinct about people
AND trUE TO his Leo Nature
He gaue of HiMself, that being trUE)
AND these quaLities (generousity.)
Will LiUE oN though fate
cut short his ViTAL Life
AND thAT of his young son
bringing them theiR final peace
& sWeet ObLiViON
BUT Bill hAD a heart of gold that
also Will LiUE ON,
AND thosE of US who arE part of
his LargE FAMILy are StUNNed
and fULL of GHref.
We all feel SUch a tremendous Loss
With juST OUR remembrances to Keep
AS Bill WAs a tremendous MAN and I
FEEL as if I'Ve LoST My DaDDy, IN. A SENSE.

A poem written by one of the SAHB extended family just after Bill's death

a lot. Sometimes he'd run around worrying about how many rolls of gaffer tape we were using, then another time he bought me a Jag for my birthday. One night he wouldn't pay bar prices for a bottle of brandy he wanted, the following night he paid £30 for a taxi to go to his favourite chip shop. Not every decision was right, but how bad is it when he was saying, if I get it wrong, I'll absorb it; if I get it right, you reap the benefits? It's great. And I was close to his son, I used to take him to football matches and things.

ZAL: Bill was a comfort zone. He always gave the impression nothing was a problem, everything was okay, he could deal with anything. He was the boss but he always tried to be one of the boys. He was a laugh, he encouraged you to do what he did. The whole thing was just so tragic. We were stunned – everything ground to a halt. And of course it knocked Alex for six – it was probably the catalyst that knocked the stuffing right out of him.

After he disappeared everything started to crumble. No one knows what really happened. The finances became a nightmare – we were kept in the dark, and while Bill was there that was okay; but as soon as it wasn't Bill keeping you in the dark, people got suspicious. Everyone started looking over their shoulders, wanting to know what was going on, not trusting anyone... his death was like pulling the rug from under everything.

TED: It shook the foundations of our whole organisation. The band, Alex, Dave, Eddie – when Bill died we started to ask more questions about how everything was being run. We felt a lot less confident in the management's ability to handle us.

EDDIE: Without Bill there would have been no SAHB. He supported the band when, to be honest, they didn't merit supporting. They cost a lot of money and there was a lot of indulgence. But Bill's tenacity is what made the band. If Bill had lived we'd be having a different conversation. He would have taken them from where they were – which was almost there but not quite – to the next level.

DAVE: I disagree – SAHB had reached a peak. Alex had been doing it for so long without getting enough out of it. Even Bill couldn't have kept it going.

THE SAHB machine was running at such speed it took a few months for the wheels to come off. But by October of that year the situation was becoming untenable, and everyone was worried about Alex. At first the latest European tour went well, with Allan Jones praising 'the musical refinement which characterised SAHB Stories, their increasingly ambitious ideas for the most effective presentation, and the emergence of individuals within the band. Currently they are performing so devilishly that one imagines they're the opening act for the apocalypse.'

Alex was taking the Hitler version of Framed to Germany, still motoring like a man half his age. No one realised the truth of the situation until it began to tell in the stage show.

TED: Zal was up doing his bit, April Kisses, on the scaffolding, and Alex had gone off then decided he wasn't going to come back on again. I got really tore into him. Alex was the guy who pushed us and made us realise all the things about going on and giving it pelters and all that, and here he was greetin' and whinin' about not going on, and I was just mad at him. Come on, fuck's sake, you can't give us all that crap for all these years then say you can't go on...

So he did go back on but he kept whimpering – Alex Harvey whimpering! – that he didn't want to be there any more. It wasn't the way you wanted to see him. Alex was the man, the fearless leader. This wasn't him. This was when I started feeling he didn't have as much control over the band. we didn't jump when he said jump any more – we were big boys now. Rightly or wrongly that's what happens to young men – there comes a time when you feel closed in and you do something about it.

Ray Conn

Alex performs Framed as Hitler in mid-1976

Things came to a head at a show in Sweden. Alex stood at the mic, muttering vaguely instead of doing his 'Good evening boys and girls' routine. The band began the Faith Healer riff anyway, and still nothing happened. They went round again and then heard the sound of snoring through the PA – Alex had fallen asleep leaning against the mic. Zal stepped up and gave him a kick, and Alex woke up, without a clue where was, and chased Zal round the stage intent on murder.

CHRIS: He was really trying to kick the shit out of him. Then later in the show we're doing the second half of the Delilah dance and Alex says, what's the words for the next verse? I say, it's not a verse, it's a chorus. And he says, what are the words for the chorus then? You're kidding... That was the night I started thinking things were going a bit dodgy. That's when we started hearing how ill he was, his kidneys and liver... All this stuff started coming out. He was on heavy painkillers as well, that's a thing – and he wasn't necessarily ill as much as he was mid-40s.

Ian Dickson

**Alex plays the
Great Dictator
again in 1976**

DAVE: He was very fit – he was a young man in many ways. He got energy from the band, from our youth and enthusiasm. He had rules, he kept himself fit – I remember he wouldn't eat a whole roll, he'd scoop out the centre. He was always up early, exploring a town if we'd never been there before.

CHRIS: Instead of taking it easier he was taking pills to kill the pain. He was exercising less, trying to take more drink and drugs to cheer himself up because the pills were getting him down....

ZAL: It wasn't apparent that he was going downhill. It was gruelling, there was a lot to do, and everyone else was busy indulging themselves, having a good time – it didn't occur to us that Alex wasn't having a good time, and that he was doing a lot of drinking in his room... It's a fact of history, the torment of leadership – you'd have Roman emperors shouting the odds in the Senate then going home to their wives and crying their eyes out... He was maybe going through the same thing. He'd been in Hamburg, worked all night – the story about how drummers began the beat music. He'd done the hours, put in the shifts and worked hard. But then we started doing the big tours, albums back-to-back, gigs back-to-back. It took his toll.

EDDIE: He'd loved Les dearly, and then he lost Bill too. As the information improved from the management he was aware of massive earnings, while he wasn't earning massive amounts. These factors led him to become extremely cynical and suspicious, even of the band to some extent. He did change. He became angry.

DAVE: He would just blow gigs because he got angry and vicious. He turned his back on the humour and warmth. It was one of the reasons I left the setup, after I had a blazing row with Alex in a hotel foyer. You're so attached to what the thing was, and then to watch Alex going up there and destroying it... I couldn't handle it.

Z A FEMALE BOTTOM IS A THING OF JOY
ZAL ON THE PENTHOUSE TAPES AND SAHB STORIES

THE PENTHOUSE TAPES reminds me of a pompous bunch of tarts eagerly regarding their own pouting arses. In most respects it's totally redundant except for Dave's moments of production genius, which has a certain crudeness that I just love...

I Wanna Have You Back: No you don't! Sounds like T Rex meets Gary Glitter. Aargh.

Jungle Jenny: We should release this today – it's a hit! A bit like the Beastie Boys meet Crocodile Dundee. Groin-gripping adventure rock. One of the funniest songs ever recorded.

Runaway: Alex again revisits the parody of his ego.

Love Story: Again a great version that manages to weave its way beyond the pouting arse.

School's Out: For me it's one of the most redundant tracks on the album. Although it appeals to the senses it's nowhere near as good as the original – so what's the point?

Goodnight Irene: This kind of shit always intrigues me. There's something about the beans and campfire routine that never fails to appeal... Nevertheless, remember those Tear Gas fans in the bath, grinning like mummies, the blood pouring from their veins... The track swings like fuck, mind you.

Say You're Mine: All the above with knobs on.

Gamblin' Bar Room Blues: What can I say? I try to stab Alex and he shoots me. I lay there for three minutes until the spotlight eventually finds me. Miraculously I'm still alive and silently shimmy up a drainpipe when suddenly a guitar floats over a brick wall. It's Alex being a cunt! I *need* that guitar. After some pantomime exchanges he finally trades me the guitar for a black leather jacket – cunt! Anyway, I'm home and dry and end up playing a virtuoso rendition of April Kisses. That was the Christmas Shows.

Crazy Horses: See School's Out.

Cheek to Cheek: A bottom, especially a female one, is unquestionably a thing of joy. Then, when asked about messing around in musicals, Alex would often say, 'I've never fucked arse and I'll never do it again.' Joking aside, I really do think of him as I listen to this track.

SAHB STORIES is *the* album for all SAHB conscripts. There are melodies and tunes like poisonous snakes licking the scented air – sweet, sensuous, stringy things, slipping up and down to the sound of scraping fingers on rosewood. Clenched teeth, numbing the pain... It's music from afar! But when the stage is cleared and the cartoon arses put to bed for the night, you just couldn't help thinking it was all a prearranged plan: the helping-hand to oblivion...

As the blood begins to course calmly and gently, and something awe–inspiring sits silently beside you, the first rule is *get yourself in tune*. From wherein you hang on to the almighty, smirking ambiguity... Curtain down. Laundry up. Time to skoosh the brew! Time for Alex to take a break...

Dance to your Daddy: Zepplinesque riff gets us back to something like a rock band. More guitar please!

Amos Moses: It may harp back to the beans and campfires but, chrism, it goes – especially live. And to think that solo was played through a Fender Champ.

Jungle Rub Out: One of my all time favourite SAHB tracks. I know that sounds strange when you consider that we never ever played it live. But own up – if you were in a lift and this came pumping out the speaker, what would you do? Exactly: rip off your shorts and show her what's what!

Sirocco: Wife of Vambo, and the first mother of reflected light. Sirocco turns out to be a woman of extraordinary courage. Follow her torment in Hail Vibrania.

Boston Tea Party: Not much to add – a SAHB classic!

Sultan's Choice: A fave track with belly-dancers and tight-lipped Sam-the-Shams from Yoker!

$25 For a Massage: Chris and I sat in his garage, him on bass, me playing drums and guitar, and thumped out this little ditty. Another all-time favourite, recorded live.

Dogs of War: No wonder some people thought SAHB were something to avoid. Here is a riff – obliquely turned back to front by Ted – that's just looking for someone to mutilate. It's nothing to be ashamed of, but, by fuck, it sure loosens yer teeth! Get a load of the Spanish Harlem somewhere in the outro...

Chris, Alex and
Zal in classic
lineup in the
mid-70s

6 ROCK DRILL

PROOF of the high regard in which Alex was held is all over the press during that difficult October. Scandalmongers could have gone wild, speculation could have been rife, rumours could have been multiplied and complicated. Instead, though, the column inches spoke of overwork, nervous exhaustion and the fact that Alex had managed to continue the show in Sweden – which led to a worse collapse at the end of the set.

Finally, though, the almost-constant grind was over. Alex was flown home under sedation and received 24-hour medical attention. The rest of the tour was cancelled and SAHB announced they would not perform again until he had completely recovered: 'probably well into the new year, and maybe not until spring'.

Business, however, still had to be taken care of, and Mountain came up with an alternative operation: the band release an album without Alex. There was certainly some material the guys had which SAHB wouldn't use, and they had enough experience as Tear Gas to carry the project off. With nothing else to do, they decided to get into it – but it would have been a lot easier without the obvious discomfort of the Mountain execs.

CHRIS: We were advised by management there was no money being generated – little did we know how much money was being generated... But they said, while Alex is ill why don't you do your own album? We had a lot of arrangements that didn't suit Alex, things he didn't have anything in his book for. But it was always with a cloud over its head. We were told to get cracking on it, work as hard as we could – but if Alex came out of hospital the project would be immediately canned. That's a difficult kind of pressure to deal with.

TED: We had a reception to launch the album at the Kensington Holiday Inn and Alex arrived half way through the party, took all his clothes off and jumped into the swimming pool... Just to let everybody know he was still there.

ZAL: I don't know what he thought of the music. From that point of view this was us straightening ourselves up, trying to hang onto our musical ideals. It has a poppy edge to it in some areas – it's not freaked out or bizarre as SAHB.

TED: He probably thought, aye – I thought they'd do something like that.

ZAL: Yeah, from his point of view it would be far too safe. He could have done something with Big Boy, though...

TED: Hugh saw himself as the frontman, but I didn't think he was strong enough. With Fourplay we were back where we'd been as Tear Gas, only a little more mature, but it was the same problem: we're four very strong characters, but none of us is strong enough to lead the other three.

SAHBWA: Zal, Ted, Chris and Hugh (Without Alex)

HUGH: It was a lot of fun writing the material and making the record. I like the fact I had the chance to sing again – it was like getting another go after Tear Gas, although the big difference is Tear Gas never recorded with me. I think my influence is very obvious when you compare the Tear Gas records to the SAHB ones, and Fourplay's a good example of where that meets. I'd brought in elements of musicality that weren't the norm for pop or rock musicians, and the result was things became more musical.

ZAL: Again there are some good ideas but the vocal delivery isn't up to much, and a lot of the lyrics aren't brilliant. The thing is, it was another situation of just supplying product for the label. American Pie's a good rock sound... It was quite satisfying to be recording again, trying something different, doing stuff we couldn't do with Alex. But it was all very strange because he was meant to be off sick and he was never away – he was in the studio and in the pictures...

CHRIS: Yeah, Alex insisted on being on the cover. He wanted to be involved. There was no animosity at all at any time – he was behind it a hundred percent – but he just wanted to be involved.

TED: I think he may have been making sure no one forget him: Hey, guys, don't leave without me...

CHRIS: Then when we finished the album we did Whistle Test, and they said why don't we go on tour? But that was also under the auspices of a project that would be cancelled in favour of the new SAHB album as soon as Alex was ready. So we'd be doing a gig in Glasgow and ask, are we still doing Edinburgh tomorrow? They'd say, Alex is feeling better today. What does that mean? Nothing, don't worry... Well why did you tell me that then?

ZAL: The tour was just a little too downbeat – we didn't have the energy and projection we had with Alex. We became almost like a session band being on the road, playing music that was a wee bit clever and a wee bit technical... It wasn't particularly rewarding and I don't think we got much of a reaction. Everything was muted. No focus. No communication.

Setting off on their UK tour, Zal observed the main difference between Tear Gas and SAHBWA was they were a lot poorer now... and a lot older, wider and more ill. As well as their own material, they threw in Jungle Rubout, a cover of Bowie's Stay and an instrumental-only encore of Delilah, with the audience replacing 'that wee guy who used to shout with us'. But as Melody Maker reported, SAHBWA was 'a cut above workmanlike without every being truly impressive'.

Chris took a moment to defend Alex, covering for a quote about not wanting to 'crash through walls no more'. 'That was ignorance on the press's part, if I may say so – but I can understand how it happened. Alex never says anything definite. He just gives you a rough outline and you have to read between the lines. I can imagine him saying, "I don't want to tour any more, I don't want to do this, I don't want to do that," really meaning, "I'm not going to do such-and-such a thing so often".'

Alex supported the viewpoint when asked about rumours he was quitting. 'Fuckin' shite,' he retorted. 'Complete fuckin' shite. People took too much out of our cancelling the tour. It was blown out of proportion – I've never felt fitter.' On another tack he did say he'd prefer not to go galloping round on one-stop tours any more, suggesting playing two or three nights at one location instead.

Eventually he felt fit enough to return to the fray, and the SAHBWA project was duly cancelled. But things weren't as settled as they'd been in the past. During his time off, Alex had been thinking about recent history and was increasingly upset about the way things had been done.

EDDIE: Alex did the last album under protest. He did those last shows under protest. He felt it was so corrupt that a band could make millions of pounds, like SAHB did, and the musicians actually make very little. Everyone says we made nothing – it wasn't quite nothing, it was a good living, but when you look at the fact we were bringing in two to three million a year... Alex could never understand where the hell all this money went. The end-of-year accounts would show we'd brought in three million, and Alex would ask, where is it? Who's got it? He could never settle with it in his mind... Studio time was a fortune, when you were on the road you were taking five to ten hotel rooms – the cost of it all never occurred to him. He never got together with the business, and never got together with the people who ran the business.

Looking at a tour itinerary, Alex flew into a rage about an obvious pseudonym on the hotel roster: 'Who the fuck's "T.Driver"? Is this a rip-off?' It took a moment to explain the room was reserved for whoever was driving the truck that night; but it serves to demonstrate the lack of trust that had filtered into the band.

Work began on what was to be Rock Drill, but early in the process the carefully balanced relationship between Alex and Hugh toppled; Hugh quit, ending six years of collaboration with Tear Gas and five with Alex.

HUGH: I'd been getting restless for a wee while before it, and I'd been getting a perception the band wasn't going down as well as it used to. But of course I was drinking heavily and popping speed and this, that and the next thing...

But Alex said something I just could not forgive at the time. I'd turned up late because Mountain had refused to let me see my contract. I wanted a lawyer to look at it and they wouldn't let me see it, so I was running late. And Alex said, right – you're on probation from now on. I said, how the fuck can you say that to me? I've had two fucking breakdowns with this band! On probation? You can stuff your band up your arse! And I picked my jacket up and left.

He'd said things to me before – that was the kind of relationship we had. He'd once told me, I'll destroy your character... He didn't do it, of course – he couldn't have. But this time I felt differently about what was said. I didn't want to deal with it any more.

The boys all came down the next night – they only stayed about twenty minutes and had a quick stab at changing my mind, but I was clear I wasn't going to. I don't know if it was the right thing to do, but I don't believe in regret – it's a negative emotion.

TED: Hugh came in and out of a relationship with Alex. He had his own musical aspirations and sometimes Alex wouldn't let him go where he wanted. I think he felt pressured by his position in the band. They wrestled about on the odd occasion –

ZAL: In leotards, of course...

TED: ...All in the best possible taste! One day Hugh was late for a rehearsal and Alex said something about it, and Hugh said, how would you know I'm late, you never wear a watch. But as fate would have it Alex had bought a watch that morning and held his wrist up. Hugh just left, and that was it.

ZAL: Alex never had the same creativity with anyone else. But Hugh had felt for a long time Alex wasn't good for his life. I remember them wrestling on the floor in Tennessee – I must have burst out laughing, it seemed so ridiculous.

CHRIS: A doctor once told us that what we might call hard work Hugh might call pressure. He was experimenting with a lot of things. He was trying to be a vegetarian but his idea of vegetarianism

The 1977 SAHB lineup: Tommy Eyre, Alex, Chris, Ted and Zal

was a cheese salad from Watford Gap services – and a bottle of red wine – and as any veggie knows that doesn't give you the nutrition you need.

TED: Hugh had a very logical approach to music, a very schooled attitude. I remember us going to see the Pathfinders when we were young. They opened up with Sweet Talking Guy, we were sitting in anticipation of this great band we'd heard of, and Ronnie Leahy fucked up the opening chords. We were like, that's it, we might as well go home now. That's an example of the –

CHRIS: – Snooty attitude –

TED: – we had, and a little of that goes a long way. Bands that don't have that musicality tend not to go very far. We got Tommy Eyre back in – he was a good mate. But from then on it changed. Any band which has a chemistry like ours... No matter how good Tommy was, it was never the same again.

EDDIE: Alex loved Hugh. Even though he would put pressure on him, he liked him more than anyone else in the band. He certainly paid more attention to Hugh, for better or worse...

While Tommy was with SAHB he managed to fit in his wonderful work on Gerry Rafferty's Baker Street, and his contribution to Rock Drill is undeniable – particularly musical phrases like the windchime-esque piano on Dolphins. But as recording progressed, it became more and more difficult to keep working with Alex.

The punk movement had exploded and was all over the music press; in fact, several papers had cited quotes from Alex some years previously in which he appeared to predict punk. They called him the father of punk, and he appeared to enjoy the title; and some of the big names of the movement, including the Sex Pistols, cited a SAHB influence.

Perhaps Alex had moved on in his mind; or perhaps he hadn't changed since the long–gone days of teenage idolhood, and in punk he found a more close-to-the-bone outlet for what he'd been trying to do and say all his life. At any rate, he found it difficult to make SAHB do what he wanted it to do – and by now there was an element of doubt as to whether they wanted to go in his new direction anyway.

CHRIS: I was asking, is it alright for Alex? Is he well enough to do this? Because I'd asked the same question about Hugh, and he'd had to leave then come back, and then leave again. We'd had to have Tommy around in case Hugh couldn't do a gig. That wasn't a great feeling for anyone.

ZAL: But recording the album was such a funny experience. From a musical point of view it was very interesting. Alex was all over the place, he was desperate for things to inspire him. He was running about with a video camera at the time – he would get us to act out all these mad little sketches, and everyone was chipping in. But he just wasn't focussed on the music.
It was disappointing – to say the least – that we couldn't manage to raise his spirits. We couldn't find a way of pulling it all back together.

But Alex was desperate to do something different. Punk was going on, and he liked the idea of being its father figure and wanted that. He got Ted to lose the drumkit and play a barbecue. He went round shooting the lights out with an air rifle while we were recording Rock'n'Rool. He was maybe trying to find something that made a unique noise. That's definitely the vibe he was chasing. Like using the pitchshifter on the guitar – I don't think anyone else was really doing that. We all went for it, we were up for it. Tommy with his atonal musical background was really up for it.

TED: Tommy brought in a different background, but he brought in the modern classical influence, Bartok and all that. It took another direction. I think we kinda knew it was the end. I felt the band was strangling me and I needed to get out from underneath it. I didn't believe in SAHB any more.

And I didn't know what he wanted me to play. I was playing an off-the-wall drum thing – which

WAS off the wall, but not enough for Alex – and he had a big long piece of poetry he wanted to read over the top of it. I always tried to give him what he thought it needed, but I was torn... I've spent all these years playing drums, trying be creative in my way, and I'm ending a relationship I'm in, and I'm being as off-the-wall as I can be, and this mad poetry's being read, and Alex doesn't like what I'm doing, and I don't know what he wants... Eventually I just picked the kit up and started throwing it around the room. And he went, that's it! That's it! That's what we want! I think Alex did that to all of us from time to time, push us to breaking point, to encourage more and more creativity. But it was getting a bit out-there. You see the Rock Drill sculpture, a cross between a footballer and a robot, and that's what the album's about – very threatening, very dark.

CHRIS: It was quite funny from where we were. We could see in from above the booths, Ted in one booth and Alex in the next one – they couldn't see each other at the time and Alex didn't realise Ted had lost it! We did Camptown Races around then... I wonder what happened to that?

EDDIE: Alex just wasn't interested at all. It was all getting quite mad. We spent more on having fun than recording the album. It was the party before you abandon ship.

DAVE: Some great music, though – fabulous stuff.

They took time out to play the Jazz-Bilzen festival in Belgium, where Alex started the show naked because he'd been wading in a pond as he heard the band start up on stage. And they made a third appearance at Reading, where Alex performed Framed as Jesus, and dropped his papier mâché cross which thumped DJ Alan Freeman on the head. Both gigs were well-received, though – especially Reading, where the band had made history four years previously, and where the poor weather meant the audience were in the bag. No one present knew it, but Reading was to be SAHB's last gig.

CHRIS: Alex was really good and we went down well. That last Reading show was the time I appeared on a skateboard and forgot how to stop it, so I was waving to everyone as I came on, then I just kept going off the other side... And I had to walk back on like a right prick...

TED: We came back from the Bilzen and Alex wanted us to go to the Vortex, one of the first punk clubs, but everyone said no... He wanted us to take on a new identity which I found absurd.

ZAL: For a change!

TED: It was like he was saying, let's pretend not to be able to play any more, let's regress... Let's play this energy-aggressive music without being musical about it. We could see what was happening but we couldn't go that way with it.

So Alex went to the Vortex anyway, and took the pipers with him, and did the Gallowa' Hills, and the crowd were spitting at him... He wanted to be right in the middle of that, on top of what was happening. It's an incredible contradiction from what we were doing with Rock Drill...

ZAL: It smells funny. There's a cutoff point. You can't go back after ten years of doing what we'd done and start thrashing around with one chord. We'd said that, done that, and it wasn't going to be new – and it wasn't going to be good. The energy was fantastic, and punk had nothing to do with what had happened before, and that was brilliant. It was needed. But we couldn't associate with that.

The pressures of time were coming to bear again. Dave was busy producing other bands for Mountain, so SAHB were producing Rock Drill themselves, and were told they had five days to do it. Chris and Ted took sleeping bags to the studio and worked round the clock. They finished the job on time even though it wasn't what they wanted. Then Mountain listened to the album, decided

SAHB's last show: Alex at Reading, prior to dropping the cross on Fluff Freeman

it wasn't good enough and got Dave back in to remix it. The escapade was yet another kick in the stones for the band, who would have preferred to use those five days re-recording material they felt could have done with it.

TED: We were under constant pressure to get things done and so most things were half–baked.

CHRIS: We were nipping in between tours to make an album of stuff we'd been writing in between gigs. There's only so long you can do that before you think, fuck this – no matter how good the band is. And we didn't have any time for the management any more. I remember when we did the Christmas gigs and we saw a model of the set they were going to build. It would cost £1500, they said. I said, that's pretty cheap. No, they said, the model cost £1500. The whole set cost £9000 – and then Tam Fairgrieve went round it and said he could have done it for £600.

And the Mountain office staff had been told not to fraternise with us. I invited a girl for a drink one evening and she said, no, I'm not allowed – it's in case you find out any secrets. So you start thinking, oh, there are secrets, are there?

But on the whole, the band were happy with Rock Drill – although, as ever, Zal had qualms about the work feeling unfinished. It has an unrelenting dark spirit, and even though the humour's still there to be found, it takes a lot more digging than ever before. Stalwarts of the band regard Next and Rock Drill to be SAHB's defining moments.

ZAL: Dolphins is a great piece of music. And Water Beastie – one of my favourite songs of all time. But again some of it's underdone, undercooked. But maybe you have to accept that's what SAHB was. I always wanted it to be grander, a bit more musical, and if it fell short I was disappointed. Still, some of the lyrics are really inspiring, really pointed. Really pointed.

Nightmare City is one of Zal's least favourite tracks, because there's almost nothing to the construction at all. There's a desperation to the vocal delivery that gives it some life, though, and in the middle of the song there's a lyric: *'I wish it was the way it used to be / open shirt on a long hot summer night / when the grass was green / and your dress was tight'.* It could be that this line, trite though it seems, is the most honest of Alex's emotions throughout the album: the dearest wish of someone who got what he wanted and saw what to do with it too late.

ZAL: Nah, they were just shite lyrics. Those were the lines I felt he was scribbling on the back of a fag packet – he wasn't being genuine about anything, it was just all imagery... He never came across as being romantic, although to be fair he liked the idea of Dancing Cheek To Cheek... It always felt tongue-in-cheek when he did that kind of thing.

The biggest question asked of Rock Drill is: what happened to No Complaints Department? In this heart-rending song Alex is almost painfully honest about his life: *'Saw my best friend die in a plane crash, my brother was killed on the stage... They took my old pal to the madhouse, in horror, in fear and in pain...'* and goes on to reflect, *'There is no complaints department, it's only up to you'.* The track appeared on early pressings of the album but was replaced quickly with a pre-recorded piece of crap called Mrs Blackhouse – a cheesy heard-it-all-before tirade against social decency campaigner Mary Whitehouse. The job was done in such a hurry that Rock Drill sleeves still list No Complaints, while the vinyl actually carries Blackhouse.

CHRIS: It's a very touching piece, it's all true, it's real proper blues. Alex genuinely cried when he did it, but he insisted it went on. I don't know what happened to it. Someone suggested Bill's wife might have pulled the plug on it, but I do not see that at all. There must have been some political reason. 'My best friend died in a plane crash' – that's the reference to Bill. How could anyone object? So I don't know – and I don't know why Mrs Blackhouse ended up on there either.
ZAL: That's people sticking their oar in for ye.

Rehearsal commenced for the Rock Drill tour in Shepperton Studios – and a young Michael Schenker would sneak it to hide behind amps and listen to the band work. Alex hired a translator, he said, to teach him 'Let me put my hands on you' in sixteen languages, although the tour was only visiting four countries. After three days of 'work' with the translator and none with the band, it became obvious he was just skiving, and the band called him out. His response was to recover his leadership pose and call a production meeting.

CHRIS: He clapped his hands together and said, right, production meeting. Band, PA crew, lighting crew, roadies, truckies – we were all round in a circle of about 35 people, and Alex in the middle with his cane. Zal comes up to me shaking a beer can and hands it to me. Alex is giving us a lecture, listen up, pay attention, I want to make this very clear... And I open the can. All the beer shoots into the air, about 20 feet, and everyone's watching it fly. We're all mesmerised, including Alex, as it starts to come down and drops on his head! And he's so mesmerised he's still watching as the rest of the beer follows, the whole canload, and all splats him on the head. Right, he says, the meeting is cancelled!

But Zal knew, I knew, Ted knew: the tour was never going to happen. Alex was in no fit state to do it. He looked ill, pale, jaundiced... Even if his head was alright, his body wasn't. It would have taken a personal trainer, no drink, a special diet, steroids, weeks of preparation... it was never going to happen.

The following morning, sitting on the drum riser at Shepperton, Alex told Ted: 'I can't do this any more'. Ted shook his hand and said, 'It's been fun, Alex,' and watched him leave, then went to tell the guys it was over.

EDDIE: It was the final rehearsals for a BBC2 appearance, and after that the band were booked for a Scandinavian and European tour. It was all done and dusted, the sponsorship was arranged, everything was ready. The agents, the sponsors and the record companies were very nervous because they knew Alex had problems. We'd gone round and assured everyone Alex was back, we'd done Bilzen, we'd done Reading, there was a new album.

So it was the final rehearsal and I was looking for Alex, and I was told he'd got in a taxi and left. He was given to impulsive things like that, so I jumped in a taxi and went to his home in East Finchley, and he said he had left because he'd seen a purple light, and that was a sign not to cross water. I thought, I don't believe what I'm hearing; and Trudy supported this, which was more unbelievable. Plus, we'd crossed the Thames twice anyway...

The guy at this time is absolutely straight, no drink, no drugs, and I tried to deal with him, coerce, threaten, cajole; I called Derek Nichol, who was on a ship in the Bahamas. Nothing could convince Alex to play. I offered to pay him cash on a daily basis for the whole tour – you have to understand the penalties for cancelling this tour were serious. Nothing would convince him. He was very relaxed and very straight when he did this. He was the man who closed the band down, and he did it the way you close a book. Completely emotionless. All the years that had gone before were gone. No tears, no emotions, that was it, it's over, goodbye.

The financial penalties were terrible. The company took injunctions on all the band to seize certain assets. I said I'd give them the injunctions personally – I didn't want some third party handing them out. I gave Alex his when he was out walking his dog: I said, I have a letter for you. That's a bit sneaky of me... But he opened it and read the injunction. It was signed by a baron, and he just observed he'd never received a letter from a baron before, and he'd frame it. It meant nothing – nothing fazed him, he was safe.

He obviously had intentions of doing other things, and he subsequently did; but he was very calm about closing down SAHB. Strange, isn't it? He didn't want any association with the management at all. I mean we were friends, but...

I only saw him once after that, when I booked the New Band to headline Daft Friday at Glasgow University. It was dreadful. It was so sad to see a man who had once been great... His performance was terribly angry, really offensive and arrogant. What he was and what he could have been... He'd been right. Maybe I should have closed the book as well.

CHRIS: Bill was dead, none of us liked the management situation... we'd never earned enough money to be paid big cheques. All we'd ever been paid was something like £250 a week, and suddenly we're being told we have to take a wage cut and we don't own our equipment... It was frightening. Nazareth didn't suffer as much because they'd made it in America and were being paid big cheques, so they didn't get hurt as much as us.

It wasn't Eddie Tobin Management. I don't have a problem with Eddie. He had a job to do. He had to wear two hats, talk on our behalf and on the management's behalf. It must have been very

MOUNTAIN

This week, Alex Harvey, 42 year old leader of The Sensational
Alex Harvey Band, decided to cease performing. Poised for
a major European tour, Alex Harvey feels that, at present,
he does not wish to undertake such a commitment. These
dates have, therefore, been cancelled.

An exponent of a unique blend of rock and theatre, Harvey has
declared his intention to totally retire. Based at his home
in North London, he has cancelled all his scheduled appearances
and says he will not appear on stage again.

Alex Harvey has a rock 'n' roll history that goes back 20 years.
His Big Soul Band was one of the most respected early R'n'B outfits
and over the last 5 years, The Sensational Alex Harvey Band has
grown in stature and won international acclaim. They have won
awards at the Montreux Jazz Festival, been voted one of Britain's
best live bands, and there is even a youth organisation, "The Vambo
Liberation Front", named after Harvey's mythical hero Vambo, throughout
the country aiding old people, charity organisations, and doing
general community work.

Whether Alex Harvey's decision is final is not yet known, but
it would appear that he has decided it is time to retire.

FOR FURTHER INFORMATION:-

SHIRLIE STONE
01-491-2904

The Mountain press release announcing Alex's decision

difficult. Eddie was the best man at my wedding, Zal's wedding and Davie's wedding.

TED: But not my wedding or Hugh's... because we weren't married. We were just cousins.

CHRIS: And because you were from Coatbridge... *Mordor*...

ZAL: Thing was, it didn't come across to me that he'd quit. I thought he'd just had enough and it was a case of, okay Alex, go home and we'll see you in a couple of days.

Official statements were confused: Mountain reported, 'Alex has told us he intends to retire and never again appear on stage'; but also seemed aware that he might do something else in the future. In the press, Alex himself explained: 'I just thought, what's the point? There's nothing worse than thrashing an old horse to death. I'm doing that in an act where everyone wants me to be a 43–year–old punk rocker. So I walked out and told Mountain I was quitting. I then found out to my astonishment that after all these years at the top and after selling millions of records – 11 gold and silver discs – I'm actually in debt! But it doesn't affect my decision to quit the business. All I get these days is demands to do punk rock things, but I was doing that when I was 18 in Glasgow. I've outgrown it. I'm not angry at anyone except myself. I shouldn't have let it go on so long. I never wanted to be a superstar – I wanted to use any success I had to progress.'

The following week Mountain released a furious statement from Zal. 'I feel it should be made crystal clear how big a shock this decision was to his fellow musicians. I want Alex Harvey to know he has sabotaged a great band. SAHB had just completed Rock Drill, which in my opinion is the best album the band has made to date. I have always admired Alex, and he has taught me more about performance than anyone else, but where's the idealism now? In reality, Alex Harvey retired a year ago, and the past 12 months have been totally musically frustrating. I want to play electric music, not mind games. I

> ● I survived the demise of Elvis, Marc and Bing, but I do not think I shall ever get over the loss of the Sensational Alex Harvey Band. — MAZ, Hillend, Ednam, Kelso, Roxburghshire.

A fan letter in a newspaper after the split

have been with Alex for five years and I expect a hell of a lot more loyalty than he has shown. Since he decided on the spot to walk out of a rehearsal and retire, he has not been in touch with any member of his former band, either to explain or apologise. You don't treat fellow members of a band this way.'

In his own statement Alex responded: 'How can Zal say it came as a sudden shock in the same breath as claiming I retired 12 months ago? And how can he regard Rock Drill as our best album if the past year has been musically frustrating? I don't mind Zal saying that, and it doesn't really come as a surprise. I wanted to move on and I couldn't do it in this situation. There comes a time when you have to move on and I had to make a decision, although I didn't feel particularly happy about it.

'I have no complaints about the band. Everyone seemed to understand at the time. A slanging match won't help and I'm not going to put anybody down. I couldn't sabotage the band, because I really wish them luck, and I'll always be their A-1 supporter.

'Over the past year I've made suggestions to ease the situation but they weren't really taken up. They were depending on me too much. I think this will be the best thing for them, as well as for me. I never said I'd never play again, only that I didn't want to play this again. I've got a lot of stuff in my mind, and I'll be back. With what, I don't yet know.'

ZAL: Mountain was like, who's next in line to say something? Zal, you'd better say something. There was some pressure about that. It didn't feel it at the time but maybe I was brutally honest – it must have just seeped into my head that it wasn't happening, the rug was pulled. His reply was great... I think things were taken out of context, I could see the contradiction he pointed out. But it came down to this: I did love the stuff we were doing, I did want to keep going, but working with Alex at the time was very shaky ground. So it may have been a bit naïve, someone maybe asked me a question and I just answered it, and that's what came out as a press release. But I never felt disconnected from Alex. I never felt we'd fallen out – I never felt any of us had fallen out. If that's what he wanted to do then fair enough, but we could and should still have been doing things... and if he wasn't well, we could have found a solution.

The European tour and following UK dates were officially cancelled at the end of October 1977. And that was the last bit. Without a band to support it, and without much label investment to promote it, Rock Drill was doomed; which is a shame since it's a thunderously impressive piece of rock noise.

ROCK DRILL–COMING SOON.

Promo for the last album

SADLY, it wasn't Alex's only vinyl flop at the end of his best years. Always obsessed with the Loch Ness Monster, he'd come up with the concept of putting a book about the myth on disc, and the result was Alex Harvey Presents... The Loch Ness Monster. It was the first time compilation giants K–Tel had been persuaded to release a new recording. And it might have worked, too, if K-Tel hadn't gone bust just after the records were printed up.

But the collaborative team of Dave, Eddie and Hair-era pal Richard O'Brien remember the project fondly, and it's another one of those SAHB rarities that's worth its weight in whisky if you happen to own a copy.

DAVE: It was totally Alex's idea. He had this vision that if he could get in among the locals, and do interviews on cassette, and do a book on record, he'd have a product ahead of its time. It was more of a business plan – he was thinking, this is an idea that could go places. If we do this, and put all these things on cassette, people will go out and buy it... Like most things, people went a hundred percent with what Alex suggested. I was right into it... We all went up to Loch Ness, Alex's family, my family, Tam Fairgrieve. It was like a holiday – it was great. He would go round and I followed with a good-quality recorder and a couple of condenser mics.

At the back of their minds everyone was thinking, what the fuck... But now it's not a zany idea at all – audiobooks are all over the place. Maybe the subject was wrong, maybe Alex Harvey shouldn't have been doing it, but I think it was just timing. The idea was sound. But it came across as an oddity – the brick wall came when he was trying to get people behind it. No one knew how to promote it – it needed a bit of a twist and they were just hoping Alex's name would sell it. I think people thought, let him do it, keep him happy; and no one latched onto the idea and how good it was.

EDDIE: The management saw it like this: every artist has a strange period. And it was viewed as a very strange period, where a few families got together with a quarter–ton of dope and didn't come back for three months... The final product was wonderful, a top–quality gatefold album with a map.

But then K-Tel went bust before it had been distributed. So Mountain had a mountain of these records, which I ended up distributing to all the tourist shops in a vain attempt to get rid of them. Every shop on the A9 which had half a chance of foreigners coming in were given a batch of them. If K–Tel had continued they would have done well with the album. They didn't look on it as a charting album, they saw it as an item that would sell over a period of time, a novelty album that would last. And it would have. Somewhere in London there's a cellar with 20,000 Loch Ness albums in it...

Richard O'Brien recalls: 'Alex was fascinated by the whole thing, especially the famous surgeon's photograph – which was later proved to be a phony. And of course, now they've tested the water in the loch and they know it wouldn't sustain a creature of that size, and it'll probably turn out to be a sturgeon or something.

'It's quite tragic – there were a number of eyewitnesses, very sane people with gravitas... There was a priest who saw the head of the water–horse come out of the water, stare at him and dive down again. And you know, that's a rational man speaking – how can it not be so? And that was part of the fascination. There was always a magical wish, and it was quite childlike. The mystical magic of "if" is always fascinating. I think that's part of the eternal adolescent which most people in rock'n'roll are. I don't think Alex ever grew up.

'It's the sort of project that would be done on television today – I can see Channel 4 picking it up quite quickly. But there were still people taking chances in the record industry. Not so much today. I remember one review that said I was delivering the narration in BBC tones, and I think it was meant to be a put–down but I thought, my mother would love to read that!'

In happier times: a collectable poster shows Chris, Alex, Ted, Zal and Hugh (at front) in happier times

A FUTURE THAT NEVER WAS Z

ZAL ON ROCK DRILL

AND finally we come to the legally ingested Rock Drill. What can I say about this album that doesn't sound too much like rapture? Rarely does something come full-circle in a lifetime, but when you think back to Framed, here's the perfect finale to SAHB's chiming history.

Rock Drill: A taste of the future that never was. I doubt if the band had played anything with as much dramatic assurance as in the opening suite of this album. When musicians indulge themselves it's seen as pretentious or fanciful, but the way this album opens never fails to bring me out in a sweat.

The Dolphins: Alex's genius abounds in a lyric dripping with indelicate references. This track is without doubt my all-time favourite SAHB concoction. Forget punk, forget pop, forget Abba. This is bone-chilling intensity that just keeps on coming at you until we get *this*: 'Where were you, little man, when I laid down the foundations of your universe?'

Rock & Rool: Grab some flowers, stuff them into your vest and give her a call! Forget the misadventures in the arrangement, the album's full of them; it's still a honking riff...

King Kong: Alex was like a boy scout when we arranged this. Out came the rifle, everyone ducked and still no fucker had the good sense to film it.

Booids: Insect tribe hostile to the forces of Vibranian repression. These are the good guys, remember!

Who Murdered Sex?: Tommy, bless him, delves into the spirit of SAHB with his abundant spirit and a genuine feeling for the absurd. A middle-eight to die shagging for!

Nightmare City: Hurriedly recorded as if someone was desperate to take a holiday or book in for some lateral therapy. Straight-jacket anyone?

Water Beastie: The chorus was recorded on a cassette in Chris's garage and welded to the studio track. Even though this was the band's last album, Hugh's theme at the end still seems to point the way forward. Here was SAHB in a garage recording on a cassette player, making music as we always did: out of the simple elements around us. It worked from day one and it still works today. And what better way for Alex to end the story by pleading with us to have sympathy for the monster...

PART THREE

AFTERMATH

No matter
what I did
it was never
as good as
those SAHB
years

Zal in Glasgow
in 2003

1 MANY ROADS

AFTER a short time off Alex set about forming a new band. Despite press releases he was always clear he'd never had any intention to retire: 'I'm an entertainer – what else am I gonny do?' he inquired. This outfit stayed underground for a while, though, evading potential lawsuits from the now-litigious Mountain.

Without an income, Zal looked round for something that might pay as much as rock stardom had. He drove down to his local taxi hire company, asked for a gig, and became a cabbie.

ZAL: I'm sitting down the office and I get a hire for an address near where Alex lives, and sure enough it's Alex with his new guitarist, off down to do a gig in Canning Town. So I drove him down to the gig, had a wee chat, and that was fine. That was Alex. He never wanted to look back.

Mountain had other ideas, though. When Alex had been ill they'd fallen back on SAHBWA; and this time they fell back on Zal, putting Cleminson, Glen and the remaining McKenna into a band under the guitarist's name. To complete the lineup they recruited ex-Tube LeRoy Jones and a 17-year-old wean from Kirkintilloch, Billy Rankin.

Billy came to the fore via his well-respected young outfit, Phase – and the ubiquitous Tobin connection. 'Eddie was our agent, and he came to a gig at the Maggie and told me about the Zal band needing a singer. We did Gang Bang, Big Louie and Ding Dong that night – I made sure of it. He told me to fold Phase, because I was as good as hired. By the way, rumours abounded I was replacing Brian Robertson in Thin Lizzy – I said nowt!

'On New Year's Day 1978 Eddie picked me up from Kirkie and we headed to London. Half-way down he informed me of LeRoy Jones. He said, but you can play guitar too, so you're still hired. We rehearsed all day but afterwards no one spoke to me at dinner, so I eventually asked Eddie if I was in. He motioned for me to ask Zal. "Eh... yeah. Sorry – great playin', man," he said. This was to become the norm in my long friendship with Semi-Clemi. Master of communication he ain't!'

ZAL: I was up for it but I wasn't convinced it was the right thing to call it Zal, and I didn't think I should still be wearing the gear when everyone else was Joe Normal – everyone's in heavy metal outfits and look, there's the organ-grinder's monkey again. I ended up not wearing the suit, but I wore green trousers and the white face and as the show went on I smudged it and tore it off – maybe that was over people's heads but it didn't matter because the whole show was haphazard. It never had SAHB's power. The minute Alex wasn't there there was nothing to fire off – there was no reason to be on stage...

Above: Zal, Chris and Ted announce the Zal Band; below, Chris, LeRoy, Ted, Zal and Billy in action

Alex came to see the Zal band, and stared at LeRoy for the whole show. Afterwards he came backstage, grabbed a whisky bottle and smashed it over a table, brandishing the weapon at LeRoy. 'You're never gonny sing mah songs again!' he rasped. LeRoy remembers: 'I shat myself... but out of sheer impulse I grabbed a light tube from the ceiling, broke it over the table and pointed it at Alex. Silence fell... Then Alex said: "Come and sit on Daddy's lap - I have a story to tell you, son..."'

Billy's first meeting with Alex was slightly less stressful. 'He comes backstage after the gig and says, "You were all shite!" Then he points to me: "But him... he's good". I was flattered, but not stupid. He was drunk that night but I got to know him better as a genuine, down-home father figure.'

Reviews reflected the Zal band's opinion of itself. Andy Gill wrote: 'As a singer Jones proved a disaster, obscuring the meaning of song after song. There was a lot of aimless, shambolic pratting round going on, mostly centre-stage. And if Jones is keen to stress that "this isn't SAHB without Alex – this is Zal!", why does he insist on dragging in half-formed ideas about rock theatre which fail to gel cohesively with the music? Part-way through the most successful song of the evening, featuring Cleminson on lead vocals, Jones returned to the stage swathed in polythene and proceeded to roll around the floor, grunting incoherently while Cleminson produced machine-gun sounds from his guitar. It was both the most interesting part of the show and the most outrageous piece of crap I've seen in a long time.'

LeRoy Jones

It didn't take long before the guys decided it just wasn't happening: there was too much pressure, too little time and no impetus. Zal decided to call it a day after a lukewarm UK tour. But LeRoy blamed himself for the band's collapse: 'One afternoon I invited Zal over to my flat and told him to bring his guitar because I was serious about working some things out. Then Chris called to see what I was up to – I made the mistake of telling him so he invited himself and Ted over. When Zal arrived, of course, nothing got done. That was my big chance to show how sincere I was – and I blew it. After that he wouldn't return any of my calls. In the end Mountain gave me a plane ticket and a little money, and I never saw them again. I wish I could take it all back – but I was young and made my mistakes...'

TED: I don't think there was enough substance to Zal. Some of the music was interesting but it didn't appeal enough to anyone.

CHRIS: It stated going in a direction we weren't focussed on. We were trying to have a laugh and enjoy ourselves but we weren't happy. It was either have a laugh or cry... I became Chris 'if it's cash I'll do it' Glen... It was either work for Mountain or don't do anything.

Ted, Chris and Billy stayed together for a short time, demoing songs Billy had written. 'Then Jim White from Mountain dropped by our houses to collect our equipment for a "stock check",' Billy says. 'By the time Ted and Chris had been informed of this, we had been dumped. End of story. After that I kept myself in London as an in-house songwriter for CBS. I had the influence to tell Mike Batt his Bright Eyes demo – obviously without Art Garfunkel – was pap. Anyway. fellow writer

Patrick Campbell Lyons had a song called The Actor Prepares that he wanted Alex to record. I played him it. "You know what?", Alex said, "that's what I'm supposed to sound like – but I'm not gonna do that." With hindsight I understand what he meant: he stood by his gut instinct and he moved on when things bored him. He told RCA he wouldn't sign his dog for the amount they were offering - £200,000... I was there!'

BY March 1978 the New AHB was ready for a triumphant appearance at the London Palladium. It was billed as the long-awaited moment that the Vibrania Suite would be performed for the first time. Only it wasn't – because Mountain took out an injunction against Alex playing new material.
    Instead the show consisted of the band plus strings, brass, pipes and drums, dancing girls and Richard O'Brien. They performed pre-SAHB material like Framed and Midnight Moses, big-show numbers like Cheek to Cheek and Big Spender - and even Anarchy in the UK, arranged into a waltz by Tommy Eyre. 'It was an extraordinary evening,' Allan Jones reported. 'Someone in the audience shouted it was good to have him back. "Ah ain't ever bin away, bebby", he replied'.
    Alex would later explain the show had been an experiment, to see what happened if he tried to work again. He'd suspected Mountain would pull a legal one, but he wanted to know how far it would go. 'It took a lot of unravelling but finally I was able to work again,' he said. 'They tell me I set a precedent or something'. In what appeared to be a gesture of hatchet-burying, Alex invited all the Mountain bosses to the show – but afterwards he invoiced them for the tickets.
    The 'experiment' story might also go to explain the mention of the Vibrania Suite – because as far as anyone knows, it never was written.
    Later in the year the New Band recorded their album The Mafia Stole My Guitar and prepared to go on tour. The press release stated: '1978 sees Alex re-emerging with a new band featuring his 18-year-old protege, Matthew Cang, whom Alex predicts to be a guitar giant of the future. Also in the band is Hugh McKenna, formerly with SAHB, Don Weller on saxophones, Gordon Sellar on bass and young Simon Charterton on percussion and drums. This mixture of youth and experience promises to yield a blend seldom heard before! This is surely destined to be the sensational band of the Eighties.'

HUGH: After I left SAHB I got a lineup together very quickly with Ali Thomson and my sister Mae. It got offered a deal but it was blown out for political reasons because a label exec didn't like my drummer. We got offered another deal through Deep Purple's management but by this time I'd got in tow with a millionaire entrepreneur and he advised me it was a poor deal, so I blew that out. I was drinking and taking drugs, so I made what might seem like ill-advised decisions. People might say it was ill-advised of me to walk away from my SAHB wage, which was probably the equivalent of £2000 a week at the time. Months later I wasn't earning anything at all. But it's what I felt at the time.
    What made me go back with Alex? Money – I had none... Alex's manager called up and said Alex had been asked if he wanted a keyboard player for the tour, and he'd said he only wanted one, me... I got very drunk and very out of it on the tour but I enjoyed working with that band. Gordon, Don and Matthew were all great musicians. Nothing was said between Alex and I about me leaving SAHB. I think we'd have got on a lot better if we'd both cleaned up our act. I know from experience that I get along better with everyone now I've cleaned up – I'm more comfortable with myself so I'm more comfortable with others.
    But by the end of that tour it got very niggly and we'd stopped talking completely. One night a guy from a record company showed up. I think Alex felt if I'd said I was into working with him again,

Peter Ball

Alex (and dance) during the London Palladium show in 1978

Ray Conn

The New Alex Harvey Band: above, Gordon Seller, musician, Don Weller, Alex, Simon Chatterton, Matthew Cang and Tommy. Below, the band during soundcheck. Right, Alex on stage

we'd have got a deal. But I wasn't really paying any attention... There was a lot of really long drives, a lot of boredom, and I was knocking back a horrendous amount of drink. I knew I couldn't do without a drink by that time - it wasn't until my sister said something I actually thought about it...

If reviews of Zal had been sour, reviews of Alex's show were at least neutral, with the majority of each article talking wistfully about SAHB rather than NAHB. When they finally turned to the subject in hand, most writers sadly concluded it wasn't up to much. Harry Doherty wrote: 'Alex still exudes that hypnotic godfather stance. His vocal is strong as ever. Legendary version of pop classics added humour. But the new songs were rather listless.'

It was without doubt the end of an era. Finally SAHB went their separate ways. Alex continued to chase his personal rainbows; Zal headed for Nazareth; Hugh got lost in the blues; and Ted and Chris plotted similar courses into the waters of harder and harder rock.

ZAL: Being asked to join Nazareth was very flattering – playing in a guitar band like that, doing these big heavy riffs again... It was an opportunity to turn the clock back and be the kind of player who loved doing big guitar. They took me out to the States so I could get a feeling for how big they were. I joined them during No Mean City and chipped in a few tracks, and we went touring then did Malice in Wonderland.

But I always had the impression money was being pissed away – doing an album in the Bahamas then going to Montreux to mix it, then living in the Isle of Man because they were tax exiles... It came to the third album and we were in Fife to write and I was thinking, this is going to be like Malice again – I'll put a lot into it, Manny Charlton will help but they're all down the pub, and I

still don't think I'm part of the setup here. Because I'd being saying, am I in here, what's happening? They'd said yeah, no problem, royalties coming in – but it didn't work like that. And anyway I wanted to try some Zappa stuff, and it was too complex for what they wanted to do.

So I went back to London and started working with Dave again, then Barry Barlow from Tull asked me to get together and we did the Tandoori Cassette thing – we moved to Henley to be near his studio. We spent two years on that. Alan Mair put Angel Talk out, but that was it. We did some gigs but ten people turned up. No one really knew each other. Dave came in but he and Barry didn't get on and it just didn't happen.

Then I got invited to do Elkie Brooks and started making a shitload of money – about £1000 a week, which at that time was big big money. But it was just work by now. Then I did some stuff with Bonnie Tyler and then Midge Ure... and I stopped after that.

TED: I went for a drink with Alex one night after Zal had split. We bumped into an engineer who knew another engineer who knew Rory Gallagher was looking for a drummer, so I got the Rory gig on the back of just happening to go for a drink with Alex. And that was three very happy years with Rory. I felt like I was being a drummer again, as opposed to Ted McKenna from SAHB. The energy level was completely different. But even though it was demanding it was too limiting in style. Rory was quite upset when I told him – I found out later no one had even left his band before.

Then Tommy Eyre got me into Greg Lake's band. It was quite good but sadly it wasn't happening for Greg. Then Chris asked if I'd join Michael Schenker Group.

Nazareth in 1979: Pete Agnew, Zal, Dan McCafferty, Darell Sweet and Manny Charlton

CHRIS: When Ted arrived Schenker had all these rules. He told him, drink when I drink, don't drink when I don't drink, turn up on time, this that and the next thing – and then said, except for Chris – he does what he likes.

TED: Yeah. Rule 27: Except For Chris... I was like, you think I don't know that?

CHRIS: There was ridiculous money flying around, and we were wise enough to watch it now. We did an album in 1981 that cost us between £250,000 and £500,000 to do. This was when the average cost was £50,000 – I mean, how many bands at Chrysalis didn't get to make an album that year because of that? We'd been in the studio for about two months and we only had three backing tracks down, and I thought, they're gonny pull the plug. But they came down and said, very good lads, keep it up... Then I realised Chrysalis owned the studio! They were just shifting paperwork around, keeping the money in-house, and they knew Schenker would be good for it in Japan... so you make £500,000 and they say, sorry, studio costs – and all they've done is generate a situation where they kept ten times the standard album cost off us. You get used to this shit...

HUGH: I stopped drinking for a while but I got into spliffs instead and started having 25 spliffs a day and got ill through that... Then I drank again... Then when I came out of hospital I cleaned up my act, but then I got into coke and made myself ill on the drugs... And so I drank again. But it's 18 years since I've had a drink. There's a chemical that generates a craving for more alcohol - it's meant to be ejected through urine but in alcoholics it isn't ejected, so as soon as you have a drink you're building a craving for more. The only way to stop drinking is not pick up the first one. I don't even think about having a drink any more.

After I'd left Alex's New Band I split up with my girlfriend and went home to my parents – I had nowhere else to go. Alex sent me the odd tape from time to time but I don't think he liked what I did – it wasn't very inspired. I was in hibernation.

Then I got a call out of the blue to play with Denny Laine. It was the guy who'd booked me on Alex's tour, and I said, great, when do you want me to come down? He said, today – you're booked on a flight in four hours! So I just packed a bag, got the flight and I've been here ever since... That's what saved me from permanent hibernation, just getting up and going.

I worked with Denny for about four months, but after that, unfortunately, he couldn't afford to keep the band together, so it broke up. I wrote piles and piles of songs and got pub work, playing old standards on the piano, Beatles, Elton John and all that. Then I was with Paul Johnson for a year, touring with BB King and things like that, and that was when I made myself ill with the spliff, so it was back to writing and pub stuff, then I joined a semi-pro band, Blue & Bitter, for a while.

ALEX 2

TIME marched on, and despite the constant work, Alex didn't achieve the ambition set out in his NAHB press release. The faithful continued to follow, but that's who they were – people who'd become Alex fans during the SAHB years. Towards the end of 1981, Alex had completed work on a new album, The Soldier On The Wall, with a mainly-Welsh outfit called the Electric Cowboys. He began another tour, again appealing to the old faithful crowds – but many of them were to wish they hadn't made it to the shows.

One of those was Mike Kendall, who'd never managed to catch the Sensational band, but had high hopes for Alex's new one. 'They were due on stage at around 11pm – but they finally surfaced at 1am and Alex was out of it. He could barely walk, let alone operate equipment. Fortunately there were only 75 people remaining in the club. The band started up but kept repeating the first few bars because Alex was all over the place. He broke the microphone stand and when the roadies couldn't fix it he started demolishing parts of the stage and curtains with the remainder. He called for a member of the audience to hold the mic for him but there was a general reluctance – and I remember him shouting, "I've played better fuckin' places than this you know..." And the band are still playing those opening bars again and again.

'Finally someone went up to hold his mic and he tried to sing, but it was incomprehensible – and before long he started another tirade of abuse. None of the crew knew what to do. They were all looking on in disbelief. I left soon afterwards, and to this day I wish I'd never gone.'

Old pal Ray Conn had been brought on board to help look after him – he defines his role as 'a kind of good influence to keep the bad influences away'. Sadly it wasn't easy, or particularly successful. Nevertheless, Alex could still shine, as Ray remembers fondly.

'We did a Glasgow date and some of the press reports were very cruel about Alex. He was very upset – cried his eyes out. And because we were in Glasgow he went home to stay with his parents for a couple of days. We went to collect him to go to Newcastle but he was in a very bad way – his dad said he'd been like that since he arrived. We got him into the bed on the tour bus and he lay there the whole time.

'He was unconscious when we arrived at Newcastle, but we went ahead with setting up the gig and all that. Five minutes before the show was meant to start we were finally getting ready to pull it, when Alex jumped up, took a shot of brandy, pulled a handstand and went on to do the best gig I've ever seen in my life. It goes to show how fit he was – but the danger of that is some people who are very fit have no reserve left after that.'

Ray has no doubt that the legal wrangles after Bill died had a lot to do with Alex's downward spiral. 'He had a lot of success in life, but he had some quite major disappointments too – other people let him down. That took its toll.'

Stefan Pawlata

Snapshots from Alex's show in Vienna, 1982

Stefan Pawlata was at one of Alex's last shows, in Vienna; a show which happened to be filmed by a bootlegger and supports his bittersweet view of the evening. 'What fascinated and at the same time shocked me most was Alex's appearance and behaviour,' he says. 'I hadn't heard the stories about his health but it seemed obvious he wasn't in the best physical state.

'At some points he was singing and shouting, full of enthusiasm, but at others he seemed to be in a trance, standing still, smiling to himself and looking as if his thoughts were far away. He would get tired and lean against the amps – and every time he started looking hazy there was a guy just offstage wearing a Roland top who seemed to be watching him intently, shouting and trying to encourage him to keep going.

'I still remember one of those old Alex moments. He wanted us to sing something like 'Freedom' for him. The response wasn't good enough, and he got really wild: 'I want more, louder, sing it for me, because this is my band!' You could see the passion and really feel his enthusiasm! At the end of this song he invited all the boys and girls to come on stage to sing and dance with him. This became a real happening – the band disappeared among the audience.'

A few weeks later, with the tour at and end, the band were waiting for their ferry home at Zeebrugge. Alex suffered a heart attack, and on the way to the hospital suffered a second, fatal, one.

It was February 1982. A marine archaeologist claimed there were monsters in lochs all over Scotland, and Prince Charles asked to see his filmed evidence. Dee Hepburn was named British Film Actress of the year for her role in Gregory's Girl. Billy Bremner won £100,000 in damages after being cleared of match-fixing. Norman Tebbit's union-curbing legislation threatened a general strike, Glasgow University students campaigned to ban topless models on newspapers' Page Threes, and the SFA wanted Scotland The Brave to be the World Cup anthem while the fans wanted Flower of Scotland. The Stranglers were top of the charts with Golden Brown, and The Model (Kraftwerk), Dead Ringer For Love (Meat Loaf) and Town Called Malice (The Jam) were in the top ten. And for Alex Harvey, the years of pushing, believing, encouraging and enjoying stacked up on the night before his 47th birthday, and it was all finally over.

TED: I got a call from a friend of mine: have you heard? Alex is dead. I put the phone down and I sat down on the bed in a daze. The phone rang again and it was a guy I knew on talk radio who asked if I'd do a phone-in. I just said, I'm not surprised, but I'm sad. Alex lived it to the edge.

ZAL: I was in Henley village hall, working on stuff with Tandoori Cassette – there was some really good stuff, stuff I wish I could conjure up now... Barry came in, white-faced, and told us it had been on the radio. The four of us just downed tools and sat there... Fuckin'ell... In a way it seemed like some kind closure. Dying before your time is a very teenage idol thing.

CHRIS: I was in the flat in Highbury I shared with Michael Schenker. Cozy Powell had heard and he came to tell me because he didn't want me hearing from anyone else. It was just incredibly sad. I got very drunk and don't remember the next couple of days.

HUGH: I was in London with my parents to visit my sister, and I was going to sign a deal with Ray Conn, who gave me £1000 for four songs. While I was down I arranged with Ted and Matthew to have a jam. But that day there was a phone call while I was out, and when I came back everyone knew Alex had died, and Alex's father had asked if I would play at the funeral. My only concern was I might be nervous and screw it up, but I didn't... I played the theme from Anthem, and my right knee started shaking and I was thinking, that's *him* doing that, from beyond the grave. I don't know if it was, but I wouldn't put it by him...

Richard O'Brien was at the funeral too. 'Alex's dad met me when I arrived. He wasn't well at the time, on a couple of sticks, and he said, no tears, Richard, no tears... And I said, You're absolutely right, Dad, Alex wouldn't like it – let's keep it together today." Then this lone piper struck up and we both just wept. Ah well, seemed like a good idea at the time...

TED: After the funeral we all went back to Alan Mair's house, and a few of Alex's mates were in one room, and our generation were in another. I went to the older guys and said, let's sing the Gallowa' Hills for Alex... They struck into a song I hardly recognised, all up-tempo and almost like a ditty, not the version we used to do. And that's when I realised Alex had done to that song what he did to everything. He'd taken it and changed it until it became really powerful. It's the only song I ever sing. I've sung it in my local, I sang it at my dear friend's daughter's funeral after she was murdered... But I thought about the song, and how many times we'd done it, and all the emotion of the moments in my life it had come up, and every moment said: Alex Harvey.

I'll tak' my plaidie contented to be,
A wee bittie kilted abune my knee,
An' I'll gie' my pipes another blaw,
An' I'll gang oot o'er the hills tae Gallowa'

Oh the Gallowa' hills are covered wi' broom
Wi' heather bells in bonnie bloom
Wi' heather bells an' rivers a'
An' I'll gang oot o'er the hills tae Gallowa'

For I say bonnie lassie, will ye come wi' me
Tae share your lot in a far country
For tae share your lot when doon fa's a'
An' we'll gang oot ower the hills tae Gallowa'

Oh the Gallowa' hills are covered wi' broom
Wi' heather bells in bonnie bloom
Wi' heather bells an' rivers a'
An' I'll gang oot o'er the hills tae Gallowa'

For I'll sell my rod an' I'll sell my reel
I'll sell my granny's spinning wheel
I will sell them a' when doon fa's a',
An' we'll gang oot ower the hills tae Gallowa'

Oh the Gallowa' hills are covered wi' broom
Wi' heather bells in bonnie bloom
Wi' heather bells an' rivers a'
An' I'll gang oot o'er the hills tae Gallowa'

3 VAMBO STILL ROOL

UNFINISHED? Right then – *I'll* fuckin' finish it.

I'm taking up the story myself here because I've become part of it, in the way torturer and torturee become emotionally entangled. When I met Ted McKenna I knew bog-all about any Sensational Whodjamawhatsit. Sometimes I wonder if I'd have been happier staying that way.

I like dinosaurs – bands past their best by the time I was 12 are the staple of my record collection. My own voyage of musical discovery was made from the wrong side of the end of the bed: but I didn't play guitar along with my heroes – I played drums.

Mind you, it was late in my life before I had any heroes. Music was something I lived with but didn't live. My first attempt at stardom was a keyboard-only collective aged 16, when my rough years of piano lessons as a wean returned to haunt me for a while. There were three of us, we didn't know we were geeks, and we didn't know we were ripping off Erasure.

Soon afterwards the notion of rebelling occurred to me – again, a little late – and I discovered the wonders of death metal. And liked it – yes, really. I bought my first drumkit for £20 and got into trouble from the Cumbernauld polis as I wheeled it home in a shopping trolley. I soon learned this death metal stuff required a bastard of a lot more skill to play than I had any interest in learning, so I looked for the passion and animal anger elsewhere. I found it in Motorhead and Maiden, and my band won a local talent competition by calling ourselves La Guerre (Lager) and inventing a hate-twisted demon, DoomDuck. (*He was laid in Hell for Satan's tea / but this egg hatched and then got free / he stole the Grim Reaper's Sunday Best / And came to Earth to be a pest*, since you ask.)

My real thang was writing – always was, always will be, even though most of the time I'd rather do anything but write. 'You're writing a book? Neither am I.' I had this fanzine, see. In Cumbernauld in the early 90s, the sheer boredom of living in an utterly bobbins new town led to a choice between two lifestyles: ned or artist. Stand on street corners drinking Fuckbast and fighting, or stand on street corners trying to be creative. Cumbernauld Theatre was – and still is – a hotbed of talent of every kind; but the council was – and still is – always trying to close it down, because it wasn't sport, and kids are meant to do sport. Seriously, the amount of creative ability in that area is astounding. One particular night the local bands did such an amazing showcase performance that no one was bored. Everyone worked, everything kicked ass – no one cared. I went home and started a fanzine about apathy.

Big Noise was a great publication. It led to new contacts, paid work and all manner of drinking sessions. People enjoyed reading it and I enjoyed creating it. As the concept grew from four all-text no-picture pages to looking more like a real mag than a zine (and you'd be amazed how many people resented that) I moved from Cumbernauld to Glasgow and started interviewing real bands.

OFFICE OF THE MAYOR
CITY OF JERSEY CITY
NEW JERSEY

GERALD McCANN   MAYOR

Citation

TED McKENNA

This citation is presented to Ted McKenna in recognition of your great contribution to the world of music.

For many years the excellence of your performance and your inimitable style have been a source of inspiration and enjoyment for people throughout the world.

This citation is an expression of the gratitude felt for you by myself and the people of Jersey City.

GERALD McCANN,
MAYOR

Citation awarded to Ted in New York when he toured with Michael Shenker. Mayor Gerald McCann later went to jail for tax fraud.

Met the heroes, talked to them for hours, put them in print, loved it. At one point it could have turned into a real job, only the 'advertising director' did a runner with the money. (Hi, Douglas!)

Towards the end there were a fair few people working for what was eventually called Noisewave, and it allowed me the opportunity to specialise. I specialised in interviewing the old men of rock'n'roll. I connected. I loved learning, I loved listening to the old stories, I loved being in the company of people who'd done instead of dreamt. And at this point Ted was looking for someone to write this book.

TED: All of the steps I took in the 80s and early 90s were good for my career. MSG were huge in Japan – the last tour I played with them we co-headlined with Whitesnake, and Bon Jovi and the Scorpions supported. Dio, Coverdale, Moore – I became part of that brethren of hard rockers. I could have gone further with that if I wanted to, but what got me was the lack of direction. Some of it was good stuff but there wasn't that quality of songwriting. I had that same feeling that made me get Hugh into my first band, and then Tear Gas. Graham Bonnet was a real nailer of a singer, so when he came into MSG I thought that was a chance – Chris and I were rhythm, Michael was a great guitarist... but it just wasn't there.

And the thing was, no matter what I did, it was never as good as the best SAHB years. I worked with some great musicians – Rory was a great man to work with and I'll always be proud of that time; but the experience of coming from your first kit to your first gig to Reading to top of the bill at Reading to Top of the Pop and so on... there's nothing like the feeling of skyrocketing like that. That's what I got with SAHB. I never got that again. Greg was ex-ELP, Gary Moore was ex-Thin Lizzy, I was ex-SAHB. Once you're at that level you've proved you can do the job and it just comes down to getting on with the guys you're working with.

Chris and I did the Naked Thunder tour with Gillan. He was a great man to work with. He makes that episode when I puked all over him sound worse than it was. Well, okay, it couldn't be much worse for some people... But Chris and I were the life and soul of the party, as usual – we both had these pairs of huge red shorts that we pulled up to our chests and danced about, running into each other like Sumo wrestlers and banging our bellies... everyone seemed to find it terribly amusing.

Ted came back home to Glasgow in 1991. During his time in Australia with Womack & Womack, who were blacklisted for not paying their band, he'd thought about jumping ship and had been intrigued by an outfit called the Party Boys. The idea was to have a solid base of a band that passing big names could drop in and jam with. In the end Ted decided not to go there in Australia, but once he came home he remembered the idea.

The initial plan had been to get SAHB back together, but it was discounted early because Zal didn't want to tour and Hugh didn't want to do any of it. So they started up the Party Boys idea and Zal was happy to be part of that. Then their bass player had other commitments, so Ted called Chris in London, who was in the studio with the Memphis Horns at the time, but dropped everything to head to Glasgow.

The Party Boys started with Nazareth's Dan McCafferty on vocals. People like Fish and Billy Rankin also dropped in from time to time. The Outhouse in Cathcart, the venue Eddie had found for the band, became the Rock'n Horse and was rocking big time.

TED: By now we were thinking, the whole smelly shoe fits... Before you knew it we had everything in place – gear, crew, everything – and we were rolling. Hugh's family thought we were leaving him out, but they misunderstood the situation. First, it was just a band that happened to end up with the

The Party Boys: Ronnie Leahy, Ted, Chris and Zal

rest of us in it, and second, Hugh had said he didn't want to do it anyway! But of course, if he wanted to do it he was in – and when our keyboard player missed a gig, that was the perfect time to bring him back in.

CHRIS: I drove Hugh up from London to do the gigs. On one of those trips, he's chain-smoking away, far worse than me, and suddenly the ashtray catches fire... We're racing up the motorway and he's saying, Chris, there's a fire! There's a big bottle of coke on the floor so I say, coke – open the coke! And he turns round in the middle of the panic and says, I'm not thirsty... Another one of those trips, we're getting ready to head back to London and he says, I know you're tired, so I'll hypnotise myself to stay awake with you all the way home. So he does this three-two-one-click thing and he's away for five minutes, then three-two-one-click again, and he's back... and by Lesmahagow he's snoring in the passenger seat. That's my Hugh! He's a listed building...

Meanwhile, the band felt they'd outgrown the Rock'n Horse, and decided to take the show on tour. People began shouting for Framed and Delilah and all the old classics, regardless of who was on vocals. There had never been a serious bid to get SAHB back together; but the Sensational Party Boys were under pressure. A lot of people decided they were SAHB no matter what they called themselves. So they became SAHB – but the 90s version was a different take from the 70s version.

TED: Dan had his Naz commitments – we'd always known that – and Fish came through and he was brilliant, and Billy did some shows... But one night Stevie Doherty was there. I knew him from Coatbridge, and he had a really good rock voice, so we went with that.

ZAL: We were trying to bring the band up to date, play things with a contemporary noise. We were

Daily Record

SAHB 93: Chris, Ted, Zal, Stevie and Hugh with a paper statue of Alex

playing things the same way, but the technology had moved on and it gave us the chance to look at things in a bigger, heavier, rockier way. The live album itself was played really well. Great performances from everyone musically – and Stevie did a great job of being heard over it all.
HUGH: There was no way it was going to get back to the level we'd been at because we didn't have a replacement for Alex. If we'd had someone who was more of a performer, less of a singer, we could have thought about doing more stuff that people could have taken to be more like SAHB. But for me it was the pleasure of playing with the boys again, being part of the band again, and proving we could still cut it – we've all moved on, we can play these songs better now. There was a lot of fun.

Stevie

They laid out their stall with a superb recording, Live in Glasgow '93, which displays astonishing technical ability and far more control over dynamics than 70s technology could ever have kicked out. It was a hard-rock angle on the old story, and while it was brilliant, some of the old guard weren't totally comfortable with it.

HUGH: We did some new stuff but it didn't go down very well when we played it. It seemed too mainstream for SAHB – it was excellent material, but people were saying, it's not really SAHB.
TED: We had done some material, we demoed it, we went to Belgium, Germany, Hamburg... but asides from anything else we were never hooked up in the right situation. There were some folk around who didn't know the script, didn't know how to deal with people. The band sounded so fuckin' good – the energy level was amazing. But the timing just wasn't right.

With the knowledge they weren't going to achieve what they wanted this time, they decided to call it a day. And a wee while later, Ted was sitting in a pub with me, talking about the official biography.

It was by no means a quick birth. We talked for years. It became obvious to me why other people had tried and failed to do the job – the guys just didn't make it easy. When I met Zal and we talked about what a big task it would be, I got the feeling he didn't think it could be done. That may have been because so many others had talked about it; but at the time it seemed as if they didn't care enough; I think differently now. But I've never known when to quit anything, so I stuck around. And got sooked in.

We discussed the possibility of setting up a netsite on the newfangled interweb thingy. We had a couple of email addresses for fans in other parts of the world, and we wanted to see how many were still out there. There was the vague notion of trying to buy the back-catalogue and re-release it ourselves – at the time, with little or no interest in SAHB, we'd been led to believe we could just about afford it (if we all sold our houses, that is).

Ted, lord love him, is not a man to use one word when a thousand will do. After I'd agreed to write the book – a three-month job in early 1998, I thought – I dug into history and found out who the band were, what they'd done and what on earth they thought they were doing trying to come back after Alex died. I realised early on they'd been victims of every kind of sharp practice and so I decided early on I'd never take a step without full and clear permission from Ted.

Thus the delay...

The website finally launched after I spoiled Christmas for my then girlfriend. I didn't have a laptop so I took up three quarters of her tiny car with my computer gear, squeezed the cat and our baggage round it, and spent the entire holiday in her parents' spare room slaving away with a text editor. I really had no idea what I was doing but I needed it to be quirky, intelligent and informative, just like the band. I settled on a graphics-heavy comic-book style format which I think was asking a bit much of the 28K modems of the time. Nevertheless, the fans liked it, welcomed it and – without dreaming of doing down the work of webmasters Wade McDaniel and Lori Reed – there was a semi-permanent SAHB presence in cyberspace.

Ted believes very much there's a time for everything. It may just have been accidental, or it may have been because we were actually doing something at last and so there was some kind of positivity about the band's memory – whatever, ex-BBC producer Nick Low decided to make a two-part radio documentary about Alex.

'I jumped at the opportunity,' Nick says. 'As a fan of the band it was a great excuse to meet them. We dug up some great archive stuff, and Lulu was very honest and entertaining about nicking Shout from the Soul Band. It went down well – the BBC were impressed with it, and so we pitched the idea to them as a TV show, and they let us do that too. It was a joy to do – but it would have been nice to have more time, and it would have been brilliant if the Christmas shows had been filmed...'

I think this was the first time I shared anyone's excitement about what we were doing. The book was an idea I'd lived with so long I didn't really regard it as real – so much so that when Ted and I appeared on a radio show to punt Nick's programme I was infernally embarrassed to be referred to as 'SAHB's biographer'. But something was happening, and it felt good.

Alex's 20th anniversary loomed. I spoiled Christmas, January and February again trying to create a meaningful update for the website; and I have to admit I made a rollicking arse of it. Hard time at work etc etc, difficult time in my private life etc etc, no choice but to do the same if I had my time again etc etc... But I think by this time there were enough people paying attention to the site for us to spend some serious time and money on it, and we didn't. Pity. (In fact we've never spent any money on it... I'll have to talk to them about that.) Meanwhile, Joe Black at Universal had been briefed to reactivate back catalogues, and the Coatbridge boy started with one of his own favourite bands. The publication of the SAHB remasters put any hope of owning our own work our of reach – but everything else was positive.

'When I was growing up the McKenna cousins lived two streets away from me,' he explains. 'They were pretty much treated as folk heroes. It was impossible not to be a SAHB fan. And as a fan and a music collector you always start from the question, what would I like to buy?'

This was the first time the band would be paid for their material's release since the 70s, and for that alone we're all happy. It also gave the band the first opportunity in years to find new fans – dads let their lads hear how it was done, and the lads appreciated it. The last few years have seen a return to real rock roots in many parts of the world, and it's good to see SAHB being an important part of that.

Then John Neil Munro published his labour of love, The Sensational Alex Harvey. 'It was a difficult book to do,' he says. 'I felt there was a great need to collate all the interviews from newspapers and tie them together with the fresh interviews I did myself. In a way it's social history – these things are lost if they're not recorded in print. It's not definitive – only Alex could have written that – but I'm quite happy with it.'

There was now a fair amount of interest in the guys again; but the band itself was still so dormant as to look dead. I was embarrassed when asked what they were up to, and I was sick of vaguely hinting at something happening one day when fanmail begged the guys to please please please just do anything. In my chosen position, having decided to respect the band's autonomy and do nothing without permission, I regularly got drunk and angry about the whole shebang. At least twice a month I got so pissed off I pulled the website down and decided to walk away. But something made me put it back up again the next day. I still don't know what.

Things had to change. Something had to be done. I wasn't going to do it, and the band obviously wouldn't either. Fortunately, Alec Downie did.

PEOPLE don't believe it, but the evening SAHB reformed to rehearse with Dean Ford, they hadn't been in the same room together for six years – and Zal hadn't touched his guitar in the same time. They really weren't sure what they were doing there either – other than that Alec had got them there.

His main plan had been to create a tribute to Frankie Miller, who was fighting the aftermath of a severe brain haemorrhage. 'The Frankie thing was one of those weird things life throws at you. I'd heard his story and thought, I regard myself as a music buff and I don't know anything about this guy. So I dug up more info and I thought, what a great story! I just wanted to tell it, and I thought a big musical tribute would be a nice way to do it. And it was...'

More or less everyone who was anyone appeared on the triple-album tribute, and of course SAHB were part of it. They weren't sure about their involvement but nevertheless, they tried Dancing In The Rain with Dean Ford of Marmalade. And it went rather well.

> **ZAL:** It was a surprise how well the track worked out.
> **HUGH:** We got this idea to treat it like Black Velvet. So when we got into the studio we had this idea about making it a bit swampy, and Ted set the perfect tempo for it. It turned out great. All the elements were there – it sounded very SAHB, with the guitar and keyboard solos.
> **ZAL:** It was Ted's idea – he knew what he wanted and it worked. I couldn't believe how slow we did it, but it was great. And Dean sang a blinder. So when Alec asked us about doing the tribute show at the Barrowlands, we thought, brilliant! Here's a chance to really be SAHB again for a minute. What a chance to show off!
> **HUGH:** I'd been concerned about my health – I'd had another breakdown in '99 and I was still a bit flaky, so I wasn't sure my nerves could handle doing a live gig. But Alec was very accommodating about it. He said he'd do what he could to minimise the pressure, so I said I'd do it. And anyway, I didn't like the idea of the band doing a gig without me...

It was a brilliant gig – quite literally, all the stars were out. I came down from holiday in a Highland hideaway, lived through a terrible train journey, had to pay to get in, wasn't allowed backstage and then had to walk home in the rain. And I still think it was brilliant, so it must have been much better than that.

It was a bit of a secret but Billy Rankin was fronting the band that night; which put paid to some of the Nazareth fans who were making catty comments to him. Naz and SAHB were the undoubted stars of the evening. The crowd responded to Billy's careful respect for the memory of Alex, and of course went wild as the rest of the guys did their stuff.

Billy reckons he'd spent hundreds of hours on stage over the years as an Alex impersonator, 'trying to make the impossible work. But at Frankie's gig we got it as right as it could be. SAHB breathed again – even Eddie was smiling!'

Martin Kielty

Recording Dancing in the Rain: above, Chris in the recording room; right, Zal and Tam Fairgrieve; below, Ted's 'Locarno trousers'; below right, Hugh jamming

Above, Ted and Zal recording; below, Chris, Zal, Dean Ford, Ted and Hugh in the studio

Martin Kielty

The Frankie Miller tribute: above, Hugh, Chris, Dean , Zal and Ted
soundcheck; below, Billy watches as Chris, Zal and Ted go through a few moves

Above, Dean, Chris, Zal and Billy encourage audience participation; below, Billy leads the crowd through Delilah

Martin Kielty

Back on the road, 2003: top, Chris, Billy and Zal in Aberdeen; above, manager Alec and Hugh in the studio; middle right, Billy tuning up; lower right, Zal, Ted and Chris rehearsing; opposite page, Zal

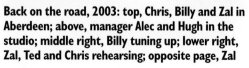

Mike Drew

NATURALLY, then, the idea of getting the band back together became a talking point, and it resulted in me, Alec, Ted and Zal sitting in a pub, knocking ideas around. The result was tentative plans for a tribute album like the one Alec had done for Frankie, with guest singers putting their own twist on SAHB songs. Ted had been talking about the idea for years and was very up for it. Like the book, it seemed like a massive project, and now I think I had the attitude to Alec that Zal had had to me a few years previously.

Nevertheless, we were SAHB (2003) Ltd, and set about organising a tour to see how many people still cared. The result was three magical nights in August, with Billy at the front and everyone else at his station. Somehow I ended up running the merchandise stall rather than taking as many photos as I'd have liked. Somehow I ended up being paid £2.50 for the week. But somehow we turned in three magical evenings of kick-arse entertainment, each better than the one before.

Brian Hogg came to King Tuts in Glasgow. 'They were absolutely amazing that night. Zal was absolutely there – just *there* – and he was loving it so everyone else did. It made me think, fuck, I wish I'd seen them with Alex, clearly enjoying it and taking everyone along with them. Billy is very aware he's not going to step into those shoes and it's his way of dealing with it to say, I'm not Alex, I'm singing these songs and playing these tunes, but I'm not anyone else but myself. I think he does it really well. I think he got a lot of respect for that.'

Work on the tribute album began, and plans were laid for a Christmas tour. It seemed to be all working rather splendidly, but then the wheels started coming off. There were disagreements over what the band wanted to do and how. I felt people were doing a lot of talking and not much listening – but that's not an easy thing to counter because it's not as if adding more talk will help...

The result was that the Christm-ass tour, as we called it, didn't quite go to plan. The audiences had a great time again, but the band didn't, and no one seemed to be looking to see what to do about it. In particular, Alec and the musicians seemed to be starting to pull in different directions. It wasn't anyone's fault, but no one was communicating the problems.

ZAL: I had the flu the whole time, but as well as that I never managed to get on top of it the way I'd have liked to. There was that feeling, this is way it's always going to be now, not being professional musicians any more... You know right away, the minute you fire up Faith Healer. If it ain't happening in the first chord you start thinking, what am I doing here, just let me go back to bed... And there was some animosity between some people and I didn't even know about it.
HUGH: I knew a little about it but only one side, which isn't a good place to judge from...

The shame was, the backstage crew were coming together, I was meeting a lot of people who'd spoken to me through the website over the last few years, and the feeling was good. Sadly, neither Alec nor the band were sharing it fully. There were some great moments, but there wasn't enough fun to justify the hassle. Although, Alec disagrees. 'I don't think there was too much hassle, but they aren't the easiest band in the world to work with,' he says. 'The original idea was to do the album then do a show – not do a tour. But it was obvious I needed to get them match fit. And we needed to raise some money because we needed recorded material to sell the album concept.

'But it's easy when you're sitting in the house to say, we'll go to Aberdeen, be three hours in the coach, four hours hanging about then three hours in the coach back. But when you're in your fifties and you've done it all before, with more luxuries like a big dressing room, a hotel and all that, it's difficult to get motivated. When you're a kid you're hungry for it and it's different – but if in your head you want to have your feet up in front of the telly, there's no way on earth you're going to convince yourself you want to be in the middle of a snowstorm in Aberdeen...

THE last straw came during a show we added to the tour in a wee pub in Paisley. Due to the communication issues we all thought we were doing the show for different reasons. A thank-you to fans; a financial top-up to balance the books; a try-out for a guest singer – take your pick. As it happened, it was as good a gig as it could have been in that environment – Hugh, for one, loved it – but it wasn't a good feeling.

It needed to be fixed, because we were starting to make plans for touring Europe, and as we began to fine-tune them more and more interest came in from other parts of the world. I decided I'd better open my gub. My feeling was that, within reason, the band should get everything their way, but I'd also realised that some of them weren't actually going to tell anyone what their way was.

In a series of phone calls I suggested to everyone that we had to work on the communication problem now. It was top of the list. I could see a number of situations that simply shouldn't have

arisen, and had only done so because even the most basic of communications was beyond us. We'd build a good team who had been able to absorb a lot of the issues, but the ones we didn't know about, the ones the band should have been discussing, were blowing holes in the organisation.

The solution, I said, was reasonably straightforward: the musicians should go away and decide what they wanted to do next, then Alec and I would work out how much of it was achievable, we'd compromise, then all move ahead reading from the same hymn sheet. But by this time our communication was utterly arsed. Ted, Chris and I spent a while trying to patch it back together. It wasn't easy – a lot of harsh things were said – but in the end we felt we'd done it. We only had to smooth a few things over with Zal and Alec. It didn't work with Alec.

'I wanted them to work for themselves,' he says. 'They had a chemistry and it was going to happen. But the reality is I had a distinct timeframe to do this, and they put the timeframe out by months. Also the Frankie people hadn't paid me and that hurt me financially. But if anyone questions my commitment I have to point out, I should be in Bali by now! That was my life plan, and I put it on hold.' Sadly, I agree – no one's commitment was in question. But there was some question over the ability of several people to listen and understand other points of view. This is a band which knows the hard end of the business 30 years deep, and that's a man who had flair and drive for getting difficult things done. There was a middle-ground, it could have been reached, but it wasn't. I think it's more of a shame than anything else.

SAHB has been around for 32 years. It survived the worst excesses of rip-off rock management. It survived splitting up. It survived the death of Alex. It survived through the sheer belief of the musicians in their music and the fans in their message. In my opinion that stood for something, and I was not going to let it drift away like a wet fart. After nearly seven years aboard this troublesome ship, I became its captain.

It was the only answer to the question. Why did we keep trying? Why did we care? Why, no matter how often things went wrong, did people keep coming back for more? Why, when it was the most irritating and demanding and least rewarding thing we'd ever done, did we come back for more?

It's family; it's love; it's spirit. It's something more than we do, more than we are. It's something in our heads and hearts, in 30-year-old songs, in west of Scotland socialism, in the memory of a man who died two decades ago. It's the Sensational Alex Harvey Band, and if it's going to die it'll die with its boots on. And so, the farewell.

B BILLY ON THE BAND

My first meeting with Zal was weird. As he isn't one of the world's best talkers I had to instigate the conversation, and the first thing I noticed was how piercing his eyes were. So I started there.

'You wearin' eye-liner?' (What the fuck did I just say?)

'Eh...yeah. Want some?'

'Sure, why not...'

That was kinda how communication went with him. I've tried to think of a time he's called me over the years. And I can't, cos he hasn't. But I've kept in touch and I saw him with Nazareth twice, with Tandoori Cassette and even with Elkie Brooks, the night Eddie said: 'What a fuckin' waste!' to his face.

He originally knocked the Nazareth gig back – 'I couldn't stomach playing Love Hurts every night,' was his polite refusal. The months of taxi-driving improved his digestive system... All in all, Zal's a quiet, polite individual – till you strap a guitar on him.

I don't really know Hugh that well, but he's an important part of SAHB. I had his Mini Moog for a while. It rattled; I opened it; It was full of vodka miniatures. He's better now, but he has a girl's bike.

Ted's the perfect mediator. He can laugh with Chris, relate to Hugh – due to being related – and play drums the way Zal likes it. 'Most drummers play to the bass, and most bass players play to the drummer', he once told me. 'But me?' he elaborated, another thing Ted does. 'I play to the guitarist. To Zal, Rory... or that German.' And I know it's true, because for a while Ted was my drummer, and the bass was laid down after we'd recorded our tracks.

He's also quite placid, except for once in Sheffield. We were all gathered in Eddie's room after a gig of which I'd played more than my usual contribution – Zal's amp was fucked. I had the joint, and Ted, already stoned for Scotland, wanted it. Everyone agreed he'd had enough, except Ted.

'Gies it, ya wee fud!' he said. I didn't know what to do. 'Run!' said everyone else. Run? Why? 'No time to lose!' Chris says, opening the door while Zal trips Ted. So I canter along the corridor. Chris jogs alongside for a bit, so I offer him the doobie, but he waves me away. 'Don't let him catch you – he's serious!'

At this point, broken free of obstacles, Ted bounces off all the walls then lunges at me. 'Ah'm tellin' ye! Gies It!'

'If he catches you he'll kill you.' Chris is most definitely not ripping the pish. I start to sprint as I see Chris rendered helpless, dashed against the fire escape by Ted's mighty blows. It was a re-enactment of The Shining – I'm screaming now, Ted's gaining but keeps crashing into corners he can't negotiate. I hear a scream from behind the last bend... He's crawling now, but the look is determined. Finally, I stamp on the spliff, hide in an alcove and fear for my life...

Next day, Ted says sorry, but he can't recall what happened. Eddie says it was touch and go. I would have been killed! The morale of this story is: it takes a touch of madness to be a great drummer.

So what can I say about Chris? He was my closest mate in the band. He was the first to speak to me on arriving for rehearsals: 'Try this, Billy. It'll knock yer dick in the dirt!' I'm sure my first try of

Martin Kielty

everything was down to him... Every night was party night round at his and Jennifer's and I was made welcome from day one.

When my dad died in Glasgow, my brother phoned Chris and asked him to go round to break it to me. He held me tight till I stopped crying, then poured me a whisky from the bottle he'd brought. Then he drove me back to his house from where my brother picked me up to go north.

He'd met my parents when they'd visited me earlier. My mum didn't enjoy seeing my squalid flat but Dad reassured her that Chris was looking out for me. As I drove them back to the station Dad said, 'He's a good lad, that Chris,' That's a pal! Chris uses humour to break down barriers, and even to get points across. One night when I'd been rehearsing with my band the Mirrors, I dropped in with a tape. 'Stick it on – let's hear ye!' he said, so I did.

He sat through two hours of badly recorded rehearsals, praising all the bits I indicated. All was well till I produced another tape from my pocket.

'Now, *this* is tonight's rehearsal,' I exclaimed proudly.

'Oh, it gets better then?' he replied dryly.

Put in my place - but funnily put.

His lively antics annoy bandmates, particularly Zal, who was too shy to tell him – but Chris knew and knows that. His merciless attacks on Hugh are going on to this day. 'You're the only guy ah know who signs on twice, ya schizo,' is one I can repeat.

4 SCOTLAND'S ALEX HARVEY

HE died in 1982. No matter how much time passes, his friends and colleagues are incredibly affectionate and protective of the man and his memory. Some people will be disappointed at how little there is about him in this book – but that's the way his loved ones wanted it, and I for one understand their position.

I often ask myself if I would have liked him, and to be honest I still don't know. No one tells you much about him in a way that lets you near him. It's obvious they all love him but they can't begin to tell you why. You wouldn't understand, I think that's their position – you wouldn't understand because it's such a personal experience.

I once said: 'Go into any pub in Glasgow, go up to a stranger and ask him to tell you a story about Alex – and he will'. John Neil Munro tried it out and it didn't work; times are changing. But Alex influenced everyone who met him or heard his music. 'Sensational' was an excellent choice of adjective. The people all over the world who got him are a certain special breed. You never forget, and I think everyone allowed the opportunity to experience Alex nowadays won't forget either.

If you ask me, it would be appropriate for Scotland – and particularly Glasgow – to do a better job of remembering the man. Does he deserve a statue any less than Donald Dewar? Should someone open a Sensational Alex Harvey Bar? Can we all wear stripey shirts on Alex Harvey Day? The situation is worth considering.

This year the Oxford Dictionary of National Biography recognises Alex's contribution to culture by including him between their covers; and Classic Rock magazine has placed him in the top 20 frontmen of all time. Next year his band take their final bows as a permanent musical force. The year after that? I hope something Alex-related will happen.

But when we remember him, I think it's equally important to remember Zal, Chris, Hugh and Ted. No one else ever managed to get the best out of Alex. Without them he'd have been a small part of the pop revolution, another one of many who didn't get the breaks. 'I remember this riveter, used to drink here, Alex was his name; ye should have seen him at the karaoke – he wuz sum'thin' else...'

Acts like the Bay City Rollers, Travis and Texas are highly regarded, and rightly so, for delivering top entertainment. But to a great extent they're functions of their chronology - Travis would be nobodies in the 70s and the Rollers would have stopped dead in the 80s. SAHB was so good it's timeless. You can't lock much of it down, and to the inexperienced ear it's difficult to say when those recordings were made.

That's what makes the band special. They're still valid today. They're still now. It's annoying to the point of painful to speculate on what would have happened had SAHB got back together with Alex. He'd be approaching 70 now, they're in their 50s... but if SAHB with Alex today were even two percent better than they are without him, fucking hell would they rock the arse off the planet.

So the time's come to draw the line in the sand; it'll be over soon. Buy the albums, see the shows, tell the world; because we'll never see the like again.

Tommy Eyre died in 2001, aged 51.
He is still highly-regarded and fondly-remembered.

DISCOGRAPHY

Compilations and unapproved re-releases are not listed

ALEX HARVEY

I Just Wanna Make Love to You / Let the Good times Roll 1964 **Polydor NH52264**

Alex Harvey and his Soul Band 1964 **Polydor LPHM46424**
Framed / I Ain't Worrying Baby / Backwater Blues / Let the Good times Roll / Going Home / I've Got My Mojo Working / Teensville USA / New Orleans / Bo Diddley is a Gunslinger / When I Grow Too Old to Rock / Evil Hearted Man / I Just Wanna Make Love to You / The Blind Man

Got My Mojo Working / I Ain't Worried Baby 1964 **Polydor NH52907**

Ain't That Just Too Bad / My Kind of Love 1965 **Polydor BM56017**

The Blues 1965 **Polydor LPHM46441**
Trouble in Mind / Honey Bee / I Learned About Woman / Danger Zone / The Riddle Song / Waltzing Matilda / The Blues / The Big Rock Candy Mountain / The Michigan Massacre / No Peace / Nobody Knows You When You're Down and Out / St James Infirmary / Strange Fruit / Kisses Sweeter Than Wine / Good God Almighty

Agent Double-o Soul / Go Away Baby 1965 **Fontana TF610**

Work Song / I Can't Do Without Your Love 1966 **Fontana TF764**

The Sunday Song / Horizons 1967 **Fontana F12640**

Maybe Some Day / Curtains For My Baby 1967 **Fontana F12660**

Roman Wall Blues 1969 **Fontana STL5534**
Midnight Moses / Hello LA, Bye Bye Birmingham / Broken Hearted Fairytale / Donna / Roman Wall Blues / Jumping Jack Flash / Hammer Song / Let My Bluebird Sing / Maxine / Down At Bart's Place / Candy

TEAR GAS

Piggy Go Getter 1970 **Famous SMFA5751**
Lost Awakening / Your Woman's Gone and Left You / Night Girl / Nothing Can Change Your Mind / Living

for Today / Big House / Mirrors of Sorrow / Look What Else Is Happening / I'm Fallin' Far Behind / Witches Come Today

Tear Gas　　　　　　　　　　　　　　1971　**Regal Zonophone SLRZ1021**

That's What's Real / Love Story / Lay It On Me / Woman For Sale / I'm Glad / Where Is My Answer / Jailhouse Rock / All Shook Up / The First Time

SENSATIONAL ALEX HARVEY BAND

Framed　　　　　　　　　　　　　　1972　**Vertigo 6360081 / Mercury 586696-2**

Framed / Hammer Song / Midnight Moses / Isobel Goudie Part I: My Lady Of The Night / Isobel Goudie Part II: Coitus Interruptus / Isobel Goudie Part III: The Virgin and the Hunter / Buff's Bar Blues / I Just Want to Make Love to You / Hole in Her Stocking / There's No Lights on the Christmas Tree Mother, They're Burning Big Louie Tonight / St Anthony

There's No Lights on the Christmas Tree Mother... / The Harp　　1972　**Vertigo 6059070**

Jungle Jenny / Buff's Bar Blues　　　　　　1972　**Vertigo 6059075**

Next　　　　　　　　　　　　　　1973　**Vertigo 6360103 / Mercury 586696-2**

Swampsnake / Gang Bang / The Faith Healer / Giddy Up A Ding Dong / Next / Vambo Marble Eye / The Last of the Teenage Idols, Parts I, II and III

The Faith Healer / St Anthony　　　　　　1974　**Vertigo 6059098**

Sergeant Fury / Gang Bang　　　　　　　1974　**Vertigo 6059106**

The Impossible Dream　　　　　　　　1974　**Vertigo 6360112 / Mercury 586697-2**

The Hot City Symphony Part I: Vambo / The Hot City Symphony Part I: The Man in the Jar / River of Love / long Hair Music / Sergeant Fury / Weights Made of Lead / Money Honey / The Impossible Dream / The Tomahawk Kid / Anthem

Anthem / Anthem (extended) 1974 **Vertigo 6059112**

Tomorrow Belongs To Me 1975 **Vertigo 6360120 / Mercury 586697-2**

Action Strasse / Snake Bite / Soul In Chains / The Tale of the Giant Stone Eater / Give My Complimnets to the Chef / Sharks Teeth / Ribs and Balls / Shake That Thing / Tomorrow Belongs To Me / To Be Continued...

Delilah / Soul In Chains 1975 **Vertigo ALEX001**

Live 1975 **Vertigo 6360122 / Mercury 586698-2**

Fanfare / The Faith Healer / The Tomahawk Kid / Vambo / Give My Compliments to the Chef / Delilah / Framed

Gamblin' Bar Room Blues / Shake That Thing 1975 **Vertigo ALEX002**

Runaway / Snake Bite 1976 **Vertigo ALEX003**

The Penthouse Tapes 1976 **Vertigo 9102007 / Mercury 586698-2**

I Wanna Have You Back / Jungle Jenny / Runaway / Love Story / School's Out / Goodnight Irene / Say You're Mine / Gamblin' Bar Room Blues / Crazy Horses / Cheek to Cheek

Boston Tea Party / Sultan's Choice 1976 **Mountain TOP12**

SAHB Stories 1976 **Mountain TOPS112 / Mercury 586699-2**

Boston Tea Party / Sultan's Choice / $25 for a Massage / Dogs of War / Dance to your Daddy / Amos Moses / Jungle Rub Out / Sirocco

Amos Moses / Satchel and the Scalp Hunter 1976 **Mountain TOP19**

Mrs Blackhouse / Engine Room Boogie 1977 **Mountain TOP32**

Rock Drill 1978 **Mountain TOPS114 /**
Mercury 586699-2

The Rock Drill Suite Part I: The Dolphins / The Rock Drill Suite Part II: Rock and Rool / The Rock Drill Suite
Part II: King Kong / Booids / Who Murdered Sex / Nightmare City / Water Beastie / Mrs Blackhouse [listed as
No Complaints Department]

SAHB (WITHOUT ALEX)

Fourplay 1977 **Mountain TOPC5006**

Smouldering / Chase It Into the Night / Shake Your Way to Heaven / Outer Boogie / Big Boy / Pick It Up and
Kick It / Love You For a Lifetime / Too Much American Pic

Pick It Up and Kick It / Smouldering 1977 **Mountain TOP24**

ALEX HARVEY

Alex HarveyAlex Harvey Presents the Loch Ness Monster 1977 **K-Tel NE984**

ALEX HARVEY BAND (THE NEW BAND, NAHB)

Shakin' All Over / Wake Up Davis 1979 **RCA PB5199**

The Mafia Stole My Guitar 1979 **RCA PL25257**

Don's Delight / Back in the Depot / Wait For Me Mamma / The Mafia Stole My Guitar / Shakin' All Over / The
Whalers (Thar She Blows) / Oh Spartacus / Just a Gigolo / I Ain't Got Nobody

Big Tree (Small Axe) / The Whalers (Thar She blows) 1980 **RCA PB5252**

The Poet And I 1983 **Power Station OHM3**

The Soldier On The Wall 1983 **Power Station AMP2**

Mitzi / Billy Bolero / Snowshoes Thompson / Roman Wall Blues / The Poet and I / Nervous / Carry the Water
/ Flowers Mister Florist / The Poet and I (reprise)

WWW.SAHB.CO.UK